The
Royal Air Force

Today and Tomorrow

The
Royal Air Force

Today and Tomorrow

Group Captain R. A. Mason
CBE, MA, RAF

LONDON

IAN ALLAN LTD

Contents

Acknowledgements

In compiling this description of the Royal Air Force I have received generous advice, co-operation and assistance from many colleagues in the Operations, Policy, Intelligence and Training staffs and at the Royal Air Force Staff College, Bracknell. Nevertheless, responsibility for factual accuracy, forecasts and opinion is entirely my own and in no way implies endorsement or otherwise by any department of the Ministry of Defence.

I especially wish to thank Mrs Daphne Stent for her dedication and accuracy in preparing the text; Mr Chris Hobson for his ability to provide or corroborate the most minute details at the shortest notice; Air Cdre Danny Honley, Sqn Ldr Cynthia Fowler, and the RAF PR staffs at Headquarters Strike Command, RAF Support Command and RAF Germany for their professional counsel; Mrs Doris Courtnage and Andrew Wilson who took so much trouble to help me with the illustrations; Miss Majorie Parks of the Air Historical Branch for her customary courtesy in ensuring speedy procession of the manuscripts; and Gp Capt Alan Hollingsworth at Ian Allan whose idea it was in the first place.

Above all, I wish to express my gratitude to Margaret who in her patience, understanding and unqualified support, typifies so many thousands of Air Force wives.

RAM

Photo credits

All photographs, unless specifically credited, are Crown copyright from official sources.

A&AEE: 120, 121, 122, 123
British Aerospace: 15(B), 16(T), 47 (Paul Oullerne), 50
Cpl R. Brewell, RAF: 77, 86/87, 91(T), 98(T&C)
T. Bobin, MoD: 108(B), 110(TL)
D. Calvert: 24(T), 136
Cpl B. Clarke, RAF: 81(T), 91(B)
B. Ellson, RAF: 84, 92, 93, 95(T), 100(B)
P. Gilchrist: 36(B), 115(T), 118
Hunting Engineering: 41(B), 42(T)
Sgt B. Lawrence, RAF: 28, 38 (BL), 39(T), 40(TL), 40(B)
McDonnell Douglas: 29, 44
F. Mormillo: 135(T)
RAE: 124, 125
A. Roberts, MoD: 131
RSRE: 126
Cpl F. T. Tomlinson, RAF: 37, 38(T&BR), 39(B), 40(TR), 42(B), 112

Cover: Tornado GR1.

Previous page: Jaguars from No 6 Squadron at Coltishall demonstrate the low level stability of the aircraft in high speed close formations.

First published 1982

ISBN 0 7110 1176 1

Published by Ian Allan Ltd, Shepperton, Surrey; and printed by Ian Allan Printing Ltd at their works at Coombelands in Runnymede, England

Foreword

by Air Chief Marshal Sir Michael Beetham GCB, CBE, DFC,
AFC, ADC, Chief of the Air Staff

Today the challenge of flying remains as strong as it was when the aircrew of the Royal Flying Corps and the Royal Naval Air Service flew in the open cockpits of their flimsy machines seventy years ago. In this book, Group Captain Mason looks at the roles and equipment of the Royal Air Force today, reminds us of the distinguished histories of the squadrons, and looks ahead to future challenges and the aircraft and weapons we will shortly be introducing into Service to meet them. Of course the Royal Air Force is not just about hardware. The underlying theme of this book, as it is in our Service itself, is of teamwork between people: uniformed and civilians, aircrew and groundcrew, officers and airmen. Together the men and equipment combine to give Air Power a pervasive influence on warfare which this book traces graphically — I hope you enjoy reading it.

Michael Beetham

Tornado ZA320 at the Tri-National Tornado Training Establishment, Cottesmore.

The Royal Air Force in the 1980s

For centuries the position of the British Islands off the shores of the European mainland has presented a dilemma to the defence policy makers of the United Kingdom. Should the country pursue a maritime strategy, or a defence policy based on a firm commitment to the Continent? Before the advent of the aeroplane a strong Royal Navy could permit the luxury of a choice according to the prevailing circumstances of the time, but those days are long gone. By 1980, the United Kingdom had been a member of the North Atlantic Treaty Alliance for 31 years, a membership which re-emphasised her pivotal position of being tied irretrievably to Europe but at the same time unable to ignore the fact that her flanks and rear turned to the maritime environment of the ocean. Those basic geopolitical factors, together with the persistent and growing military capability of the forces of the Warsaw Pact, determined the posture, structure and roles of the Royal Air Force at the outset of a decade which was, by any yardstick, to be of momentous significance for British airpower.

Ever since the formation of the North Atlantic Treaty Organisation in 1949, its strategies had depended heavily on air-power for their efficacy. But in 1967, a posture was adopted which was to have even greater significance for the Royal Air Force. Hitherto, the Alliance strategy had been largely based on the assumption that an incursion by a potential enemy, usually identified as the Warsaw Pact, would be met by a nuclear response, but, in the face of increasing Warsaw Pact nuclear strength, such a posture, however practical, began to lose its deterrent credibility, especially against possible small scale incursions. Hence, the NATO Council approved the shift in posture to one of flexible and appropriate response; a posture which still rests on the bedrock of nuclear deterrence but which lays greater emphasis on conventional forces. Since 1967, however, Warsaw Pact conventional forces have also increased in strength so that as successive United Kingdom Defence White Papers have described, NATO forces in Europe are outnumbered by in-place Warsaw Pact forces in tanks, artillery and armoured personnel carriers. Under all foreseeable circumstances the Pact would hold the tactical initiative of choosing the time, location and method of attack. The West could have as little as 48 hours in which to prepare to respond.

Consequently, when one reflects on the geographical divisions between NATO's regions: the Atlantic itself, the Baltic, the North Sea, The Alps, the Mediterranean, the Adriatic and the Aegean and on the distances which reinforcements must travel to make up

Below: Tornado F2 prototype. The Air Defence Variant of the Tornado is destined to become the backbone of Strike Command and the RAF has plans to acquire 165 aircraft.

in-position numbers, it is easy to see why airpower is of such critical importance to Alliance strategy. Only the NATO Air Forces could strike swiftly from long range perhaps from north to south or west to east as the threat demanded; only by airpower attacking enemy forces directly or by transporting reinforcements and supplies to hard-pressed ground troops could the initial enemy advantages be neutralised. Should deterrence ever fail, the speed, range and concentration of force achievable by NATO airpower would be indispensable to Allied success, both against invading ground forces in Europe and against marauding surface and submarine vessels on the sea-lanes. Allied seapower would concentrate on the battle of the sea-lanes, land power would seek to stem the advance of enemy armour on the Continent, but NATO airpower would have to be involved in both; and because of the geographical position of the United Kingdom, the Royal Air Force would have an indespensable part to play.

Below: The Commander-in-Chief UK Air was placed in a direct chain of command to NATO's Supreme Allied Commander Europe in 1975. This fact is reflected in the ceremony that accompanied the handover of the position from ACM Sir David Evans (first right) to the present incumbent ACM Sir Keith Williamson (third right) in September 1980. As seen in the photograph the flag symbolising UK Air was handed back to the SACEUR (Gen Bernard Rogers) who then officially presented it to the new holder.

Organisation of the Royal Air Force

To discharge the responsibility of British air power not just to the Western Alliance, but in support of British policy in residual areas of Imperial responsibility such as Hong Kong or Gibraltar, and to other commitments such as Belize or Cyprus, the RAF is organised in three Commands: Strike, Royal Air Force Germany and Royal Air Force Support Command.

Strike Command was created in 1968 from an amalgamation of Fighter, Bomber, Coastal and Transport Commands. In 1975, the concentration of so many resources was recognised when the Air Officer Commanding-in-Chief Strike Command was made Commander-in-Chief UK Air (CINCUKAIR) and placed in a direct chain of command to the North Atlantic Treaty Organisation's Supreme Allied Commander Europe (SACEUR). The appointment reflected the importance of the RAF's airpower to NATO and the continued strategic pivotal position of the United Kingdom itself which is, at the same time, the rear base for SACEUR in Europe and the forward base for maritime operations in the Atlantic and British waters. The Command Headquarters is at High Wycombe in Buckinghamshire, the site of MRAF Sir Arthur Harris' wartime Bomber Command headquarters. The Command is functionally divided into four Groups which discharge the responsibilities of CINCUKAIR. No 1 Group at Bawtry in Yorkshire has inherited the functions of the old Bomber Command: nuclear strike, conventional attack, strategic

Organisation of the Royal Air Force.

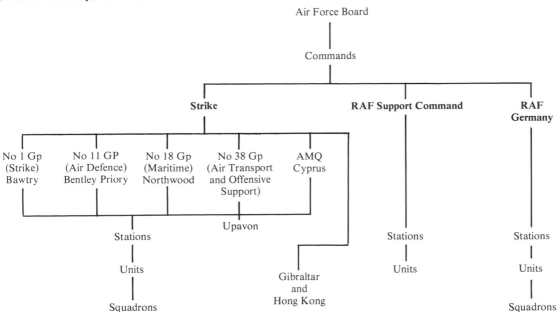

reconnaissance and in-flight refuelling. No 11 Group has the old Fighter Command Headquarters at Bentley Priory and the associated responsibility for providing the air defence of the United Kingdom. No 18 Group, commanded from Northwood, provide maritime reconnaissance and offensive roles as well as search and rescue. No 38 Group, with headquarters at Upavon in Wiltshire, is responsible for offensive support, tactical reconnaissance, strategic airlift and tactical fixed-wing and rotary air mobility. In addition to controlling the four Groups, Headquarters Strike Command administers two other organisations in peacetime. The first, the Central Trials and Tactics Organisation, is responsible for formulating tactical doctrine and conducting associated operational trials. The second, Military Air Traffic Operations, has Group status within the Command with responsibilities which include provision of area traffic control and information services in the United Kingdom Flight Information Region and Upper Information Regions to military aircraft, the co-ordination of all matters concerning the safe and efficient use of UK airspace by military aircraft and the implementation of policies concerning the operation of the United Kingdom Low Flying System.

Across on the Continent, RAF Germany in many ways resembles Strike Command. It is much smaller and it does not have its own maritime aircraft or long range airlift but it does contribute a wide range of British airpower to SACEUR's strength in the Central Region. In peacetime, RAF Germany has a national responsibility towards the integrity of the airspace of the Federal Republic of Germany and the maintenance of access along the air corridors to Berlin. In war, as part of the Second Allied Tactical Air Force (2ATAF) the squadrons in Germany would provide conventional attack, nuclear strike, reconnaissance and other air defence and tactical mobility in co-operation with NATO land forces. (The Command is described in full in Chapter 5.)

Supporting both Strike Command and Royal Air Force Germany, as its name implies, is Royal Air Force Support Command which was created in 1977 by a merger of Training and Support Commands which brought about considerable manpower and financial savings without reducing the power of the front-line. The structure of the modern Command now controlled from its headquarters at Brampton, Cambridgeshire, clearly reflects its distinguished antecedents. The legacy of Flying Training Command is seen in units which range from the University Air

Squadrons flying Bulldogs to the internationally prestigious Central Flying School at Leeming. The traditions of Technical Training Command are preserved at units such as Halton and Locking. The Colleges at Bracknell and Cranwell retain their responsibilities for professional officer training. The maintenance units which prepare aircraft and ground equipment for the Service have been inherited from Maintenance Command. Units in the one-time Signals Command, without those communications the Royal Air Force could not continue to operate and the hospitals once governed by Home Command are now all part of the Support Organisation controlled from Brampton.

Prospect for the 1980s

As the Royal Air Force moved into the 1980s, the three Commands were responsible for some 900 aircraft in front-line squadrons or in immediate reserve, with another 450 employed in various training roles. The total uniformed strength was in excess of 88,000 people. The RAF like the other British Armed Services had been drastically reduced in the previous generation by a series of cuts in provision for defence and as a result of withdrawals from the Middle and Far East. Older equipment in the Service had been designed for use during the 'massive retaliation' period of strategy, before the decision in 1967 to adopt the posture of flexible response. Some re-equipment plans had been victims of the defence reduction while others had been reduced or protracted. Nevertheless, by 1980, the training fleet had been modernised and the front-line was about to be strengthened by several new aircraft. Most important, of course, were the 220 Tornado GR1s and 165 Tornado F2s which will be the background of the Service for many years to come. Smaller in number but of great significance because of the way they increase the capability of other aircraft (hence their tag of 'force multiplier') were the airborne early warning Nimrods and VC-10 tankers. The maritime Nimrods were being updated to Mk 2 standard while overland tactical mobility was being enhanced by the advent of the Chinook helicopters and the stretching of the fuselages of a proportion of the Hercules fleet. A major weapon programme included new air-to-air and air-to-surface missiles, more surface-to-air missiles and new electronic counter-measures (ECM) equipment. Less spectacular but of great importance, were programmes to improve avionics, weapon management, airframes and engines on several types of aircraft as well as the introduction of new ground communication and air defence environment

Above: British ingenuity and American engineering — the AV-8B prototype demonstrates its independence of conventional runways while carrying four low-drag bombs.

Advancing technology promised great advantages for airpower but when aircraft could take 10 years from drawing board to squadron and remain in service for a further 20, great care had to be taken to avoid rapid obsolescence on the one hand or too hasty adoption of unproven ideas on the other. The potential of the micro-processor was enticing: it offered reduced weight, reduced volume, reduced power requirements and reduced unit costs at the same time as improved reliability, accuracy and weapon specialisation. Working in the third dimension, the Royal Air Force could not afford to neglect any opportunity to harness these developments.

Regrettably, it would not just be the RAF or even our Allied Air Forces who would benefit from advanced technology. The qualitative and quantitative improvements of the Soviet Armed Services showed no signs of slowing down. Indeed, by 1980, the Soviet Union was allocating some 12% of its gross national product to defence of which one-fifth was spent on research and development and more ominously, was devoting a greater proportion of the whole defence budget to its Air Forces than on its land and sea forces put together. The potential of Soviet offensive aircraft, surface-to-air defences and fourth generation interceptors working with an equivalent of the Western AWACS would continue to challenge the skills, determination and imagination of RAF aircrew and groundcrew alike.

The RAF of the 1980s would, therefore, be increasingly well-equipped but would need to draw the last ounce of effectiveness from men and machines to face the potential of a formidable enemy. It was a situation not unknown in the Service's short but proud history.

systems. Longer term studies were continuing of cruise missiles for both tactical and strategic use with both conventional and nuclear warheads, while requirements were being examined to determine the best kind of manned aircraft and missile mix for offensive support and air superiority tasks in the 1990s.

There were additional reasons for ensuring that requirements and provision to meet them were as economical and effective as possible. The costs of most kinds of military equipment had risen faster than the general national average and no government could afford to make unlimited allocation of resources to defence. It was, therefore, even more important to apply Lord Trenchard's dictum:

'Remember that the one great thing to which you should at all times apply your thoughts and brains is the expansion of the power of material and personnel without increasing either. That way lies economy.'

Air Defence of the United Kingdom

On average, five times a week in 1981, fighters of No 11 Group intercepted Russian aircraft which were probing the British Air Defence Region, usually out over the waters of the northern North Sea or the Eastern Atlantic. The call to 'Scramble' could come at any hour of day or night to the Phantoms or Lightnings kept at a high state of readiness 24 hours a day, seven days a week at the fighter bases in Strike Command.

Within one or two minutes of the call, the 'Quick Reaction Alert' aircraft would be rolling down the runway prior to climbing away through cloud, rain or snow to the transit height en route to an interception point which could be as much as 800 miles off the coast of the United Kingdom. It is a far cry from the blue skies of summer 1940: from the scramble of Spitfires and Hurricanes from grass fields in the south of England against the Luftwaffe bomber streams already less than 100 miles away. But although Fighter Command is now 11 Group, and Merlin engines have given way to Speys and Avons, the fundamental task remains the same: the preservation of the integrity of United Kingdom airspace. Then it was during the war, now it is during the peace, but with the added incentive that the more effective the interceptors are seen to be in peacetime, the less likely are they to be called upon to fire their missiles or their guns in anger.

The Changing Threat
In the early 1950s, the major air threat to the United Kingdom came from the first generation of postwar Soviet jet bombers armed with free-fall conventional or nuclear weapons. The squadrons of Fighter Command were deployed on many bases round the British coast from Leuchars in the north to Tangmere in the south, very much as they had been ten years previously in World War 2. Then, as NATO strategy was modified to deter or to fight a short nuclear war and as the Soviet Union herself began to deploy surface-to-surface missiles with nuclear warheads, the perception of the threat to the United Kingdom changed accordingly. The Defence White Paper of 1957 asserted that the manned bomber would be superseded by the surface-to-surface missile and there would be no need to replace the Lightning fighter by any other manned interceptor, that there was no

Below: A Phantom of No 111 Squadron, armed with Sidewinder missiles, intercepts a Soviet maritime reconaissance Tu-95 'Bear-D' over the North Sea in 1980.

defence against missile attack, that our defence posture would be based much more exclusively on the nuclear deterrent power of the V-Force and that, therefore, the role of Fighter Command would be reduced to that of protecting the V-Force bases. This remained the posture throughout the 1960s and into the 1970s.

The Soviet Union, however, saw the strategic environment somewhat differently. She did, indeed, develop her surface-to-surface nuclear tipped missiles but also continued to introduce new manned bombers capable of in-flight refuelling and equipped with stand-off weapons with both conventional and nuclear warheads. She is now producing some 30 Tu-22M 'Backfire' bombers a year, of which half are entering service with the Soviet Maritime Air Arm and the others with Long Range Aviation, the equivalent of the old Royal Air Force Bomber Command. 'Backfire' is believed to be capable of speeds of Mach 2 at height, carries a bombload in excess of 12,000lb or the air-to-surface 'Kitchen' long-range stand-off missile and with in-flight refuelling could attack the United Kingdom from any direction. In the longer term it could be escorted by either later marks of the MiG-23 'Flogger' interceptor or by the projected longer range two-seat variant of the MiG-25 'Foxbat'.

Nor is 'Backfire' the only threat. Large numbers of Su-24 'Fencer' are entering service with Frontal Aviation at the rate of 50 a year. From their permanent bases in Western Russia, they could reach the United Kingdom on a high-low-high flight profile, but if deployed forward to bases in Eastern Germany, they could significantly increase the threat of larger scale low-level attack on these islands. 'Fencer' carries a weapon system specialist seated alongside the pilot to operate the advanced navigation and attack systems which would allow it to fly at low level at night or in bad weather, with a bombload significantly larger than its shorter range predecessors in the Warsaw Pact Air Forces. So, 11 Group faces a formidable adversary and, as Soviet aircraft continue to improve their performance, its responsibility will increase.

United Kingdom Air Defence and NATO

Just as in 1940 the fate of Western Europe hung in the balance, so in any future conflict more than just the security of the United Kingdom would be at stake in the struggle for command of the United Kingdom Air Defence Region. Since 1967, the North Atlantic Treaty Organisation has adopted a strategy of 'flexible and appropriate response' to any aggression. The Alliance's primary aim is to deter aggression, but should deterrence fail, then the enemy would be met by a level of military response deemed appropriate at the time. In practice, this has implied a possibility of fighting a conventional phase of warfare to defend allied territory as near to the eastern borders as possible.

But such a strategy is threatened by the in-place numerical superiority of Warsaw Pact troops, tanks, artillery and armoured personnel carriers. Consequently, on warning of imminent aggression, and as quickly as possible after the outbreak of conflict, our land forces in Europe must be rapidly reinforced. A large proportion of those reinforcements would move either from, through or over the United Kindom. It is, therefore, of critical importance to the Alliance as a whole that our reinforcement routes, harbours, airfields, railheads and concentration areas be kept free from enemy air attack. If he were to succeed in isolating the conflict area of his choice from its major reinforcements, his local superiority could be overwhelming. This explains the heavy responsibility underlying the tasks allocated to the various components of 11 Group in the 1980s.

The Aircraft

The peacetime interceptions are made by the seven fighter squadrons of the Group, all bearing famous numbers and proud traditions. Guarding the northern flank and the eastern Atlantic sea routes are the Phantom FG1s of No 43 Squadron: the 'Fighting Cocks'. No 43 has a particular commitment to the air defence of maritime forces in addition to the broader responsibility to United Kingdom airspace. In addition to distinguished service in both world wars, the Squadron has a long association with Scotland, being formed at Stirling in 1916. Sharing the airfield at RAF Leuchars is No 111 Squadron, known familiarly as the 'Tremblers'. In 1979 No 111 maintained the standards which had allowed it to claim 94 enemy aircraft destroyed during the Battle of Britain when it won the first Royal Air Force fighter competition for the Seed air-to-air gunnery trophy with score in excess of 25% after a 'shoot-out' over towed banner targets. 'Treble-One', like all the other RAF Phantom squadrons except '43', flies the FGR2 or F-4M model which may be armed with four air-to-air Sidewinder heat-seeking missiles and four Sparrow radar-guided longer range missiles as well as a six barrelled General Electric M-61 gun. The FGR2 has an effective unrefuelled combat radius of some 500 miles with a top speed in excess of Mach 2 at height and over Mach 1 at low level, where its pulse doppler radar aids detection and attack.

Below: A Lightning F6 of No 11 Squadron over the North Sea.

Also equipped with FGR2s are No 29 Squadron and No 228 OCU at Coningsby and, guarding East Anglia and the approaches to the Home Counties, are No 23 and No 56 Squadrons at Wattisham. Both No 29 and No 23 have been in the night and all-weather fighter game since flying Blenheims at the outbreak of World War 2. No 56, on the other hand, has always hitherto been a day fighter squadron, including among its World War 1 aircrew, Victoria Cross winners Albert Ball and J. B. McCudden, and subsequently playing a prominent part in the Battle of Britain.

The other two squadrons, based at Binbrook in Lincolnshire are No 5 and No 11 Lightning Squadrons which share the task of the Southern Quick Reaction Alert Force with the Wattisham Phantoms. No 5 Squadron forced down the first enemy aircraft of World War 1 on 24 August 1914, while No 11 has had a varied record of service reverting in 1948 to its original fighter role. The Lightning has now seen 20 years' service and it remains a formidable interceptor. Both squadrons operate a mix of F3 and F6 models and the latter is capable of speeds in excess of Mach 2. It is equipped with a long range search radar and Red Top missiles which can attack from any angle. For closer range operations it carries two 30mm cannon. Originally designed for high-level operating, the Lightning continues to prove its versatility by intercepting targets at all altitudes and continues to capitalise on its very high speed and high rate of climb.

Peacetime Preparedness

The level of combat effectiveness achieved by the interceptors of 11 Group is the product of hard training and a great deal of teamwork. Day to day training will include practice interceptions which will steadily increase in complexity against targets flying at different heights and speeds, sometimes evading, sometimes not, and sometimes against a background of electronic countermeasures. In the Phantom Squadrons, teamwork begins with pilot and navigator: the latter not only contributing to the overall lookout but operating the aircraft's own target radar which in the event of heavy enemy jamming of the ground radar station could allow the interception still to be carried out. All the fighter squadrons are likely to spend a great deal of time well away from land in a potentially hostile environment, frequently at low level, and they have not only to locate and intercept a target but also navigate back to base. Nor is the weather of the North Sea and the Iceland-Faroes Gap conducive to visual navigation.

The crews, however, are not always on their own. They work as part of a broader team which includes airborne early-warning aircraft, in-flight refuelling aircraft, ground radar and control stations and, for those intruders who penetrate to closer range, air-to-ground defences.

By 1972, the low-level threat to the United Kingdom was becoming apparent. Existing ground radar stations provided good medium and high level cover but below that there were gaps. Consequently, No 8 Squadron, itself possessing a famous fighter ground-attack history in both world wars and thereafter was reformed with Shackleton AEW2 aircraft, converted from the maritime reconnaissance role as they were replaced by the Nimrod. At its base at Lossiemouth in Northern Scotland, No 8 Squadron also mounts a Quick Reaction Alert, in harness with its faster interceptor team-mates. On receipt of the news that a 'bear' is on its way from its lair in the Kola peninsula the QRA Shackleton is scrambled with an alacrity that belies its years of service. The endurance that was provided originally to allow it to patrol for 10 hours or more over the Atlantic now permits it to remain on station for several hours working with the interceptor crews, the sustaining tankers and the ground control unit, providing warning of low-level intrusion far earlier than would be achieved by the ground unit itself and, when required, contributing to the actual control of the interceptors themselves.

The third element in the team is the visitor from 1 Group, the Victor K2 tanker from either No 55 or No 57 Squadron at Royal Air Force Marham. As explained in Chapter 3, the tanker squadrons provide, by in-flight refuelling, vital extra range for several types of air operation. They permit the fighters to mount air patrols, known as 'Combat Air Patrols', several hundred miles off the British coast thereby making interception possible before the attacking bomber has reached its own air-to-surface missile release point. In peacetime, they help the Phantom and Lightning to intercept and shadow the prowling Bear well before he reaches British airspace, thereby emphasising how difficult his task would be in war. Under normal circumstances, the team of interceptors, airborne early warning and tanker aircraft would operate under the direction of the ground control organisation within the United Kingdom Air Defence ground environment. This organisation includes surveillance radar stations, the ballistic missile early warning station at Fylingdales, communication systems, sector operation centres and the United Kingdom regional Air Operations Centre at West Drayton near London. Fylingdales is unique in the United Kingdom system in that its primary responsibility is not to provide early warning of Soviet aircraft but of the launching of inter-continental ballistic missiles. It has a direct communication link with the North American Air Defence Centre at Colorado Springs as well as to 11 Group Headquarters and to Strike Command Headquarters. Although, happily, Fylingdales has not yet had to track any missile, it does keep a close eye on some 1,200 satellites each week.

In 1980, plans were announced for extensive modifications to the United Kingdom Air Defence ground environment system to ensure that it will be prepared for expected improvements in the Soviet offensive threat during the next decade. Surveillance data for an area of four million square miles of airspace will be provided by sensors operating in the air, on the ground and at sea. A network of control centres and reporting posts will be commanded from a new Air Defence Operations Centre. The security of command and control will be protected from physical attack by a high capacity flexible digital data network which will permit information flow to be switched to alternative paths. A high degree of redundancy and other methods will give further protection against electronic countermeasures. Reaction time will be reduced by modern automatic data processing and the whole system will be designed to cope with the maximum expected target and air defence resource activities. Interoperability with other NATO and national systems will be assured.

Surface-to-Air Defences

Should any aircraft penetrate this air defence team they would meet the short-range air-to-ground missile units of the Rapier and Bloodhound missile squadrons.

Rapier has been in operation with RAF Regiment squadrons of No 38 Group since 1974. It is a short-range, highly effective low-level rapid reaction weapon which is guided either optically or by radar. Although normally deployed for point protection such as airfields it is highly mobile, each unit requiring only three Land Rovers. Each launcher carries four missiles powered by a two-stage solid fuel motor. Surveillance radar, together with IFF, provides early detection and identification of approaching aircraft. Typical of such a squadron is No 27 Rapier Squadron Royal Air Force Regiment, equipped with the Blindfire target acquisition system which provides 24-hour air-to-surface defence at RAF Leuchars. In 1981, the United States Government announced that it intended to purchase Rapier to defend USAF bases in the United Kingdom. The concentration of effort will obviously be against air attacks on those airfields but the air defence net, as a whole, will be proportionately strengthened. In due course, Rapier will be further improved by a computer modification and a new radar capable of tracking several targets simultaneously.

Bloodhound 2 is an older weapon, entering service in 1964 but is still an effective medium and low-level system with well proven electronic countermeasure features. It is powered by four solid propellant motors and homes on to targets illuminated by a ground target radar. Its high explosive warhead has a proximity

fuse and its operating range is in excess of 80 miles at heights from 100ft to more than 60,000ft. In 1982, the Bloodhound units at present located at Laarbruch, Bruggen and Wildenrath will be transferred to the United Kingdom for deployment in Lincolnshire and East Anglia.

Intensified Training

This defensive blend of interceptors and missiles must be effectively co-ordinated. 'Routine' training, therefore, involves all-weather practice interceptions, QRA, working with the Shackletons, in-flight refuelling, mastering procedures with the surface-to-air missile squadrons, flying almost instinctively with ground control and confidently without it. Indeed, such training can scarcely be called 'routine', yet compared to other activities, it may well seem to be so to the fighter crews.

For several years now the USAF has maintained an 'Aggressor' Squadron of F-5s at RAF Alconbury whose task is to provide 'dissimilar' combat training to USAF and RAF fighter crews. Obviously, when the majority of peacetime RAF 'interceptions' are made against friendly Phantoms, there are the obvious dangers of combat parameters becoming determined by the similarity of the aircraft themselves. The lightweight F-5, however, can be flown in very different patterns thereby greatly extending the range of threats to which the RAF crews can become accustomed. Inevitably, keen but good-humoured Allied rivalry gives added spice to the encounters.

A further diversion occurs when the squadrons move away to overseas bases for additional training or competitions. The Mediterranean, for example, might not always present the operational challenges of the North Sea environment but there are obvious compensations in the guaranteed clear weather for those exercises which depend on visual target acquisition and clear air manoeuvres. In October 1980, Group Captain Alan Parkes, Station Commander at Akrotiri in Cyprus, explained how his unit provided facilities for the squadrons of 11 Group:
'We are busy for some ten months of the year with these Armament Practice Camps. Each squadron comes here for about five weeks and carries out its annual training with live gunfire. The target-towing aircraft are Canberras of 100 Squadron. Each fighter pilot flies a number of cine-camera sorties until he has demonstrated that he can consistently achieve the required safety parameters of range and angle-off, chasing the Canberra towing a target banner on a 300-yard rope. The Squadron Weapons Instructor then tests the pilot firing live 30mm shells against the banner. The pilot then flies six academic shoots in order to gain Allied Common Europe qualifications. This qualification is a percentage score based on hits made against rounds fired and the standard, laid down by Supreme Headquarters Allied Powers Europe, is common to all NATO Air Forces.'

Closer to home, regular missile-firing practice takes place at ranges off North Wales and North Eastern Scotland while squadron exchanges with NATO allies encourage both competition and an awareness of common procedures and objectives.

The most realistic training of all, however, occurs when the entire station assumes that actual conflict has started and, under the eagle eyes of Allied Staff Officers, the squadrons demonstrate how effectively they can operate under simulated wartime conditions. Such conditions may be applied to one station only, which is called a 'Tactical Evaluation' or TACEVAL for short, or it may be part of an 11 Group or even a NATO-wide defence exercise as in 'Elder Forest' in 1980.

TACEVAL is the test by SACEUR of a station's ability to move swiftly from peacetime conditions to war and of its capacity to fight it. The Evaluation Team will simulate just about every incident that could disrupt the Air Defence task. Aircraft will be declared destroyed on the ground, runways will be obstructed, fuel installations fired, the Station Commander or any combination of his deputies 'killed', a chemical attack received, all communications jammed; and yet the fighters must get airborne and the interceptions made. At the end of the exercise, the performance of the squadrons will be assessed and it is a considerable source of pride among units of 11 Group, as indeed elsewhere in the Royal Air Force, that standards achieved are consistently well above the NATO average.

If the station is participating in a broader NATO exercise, more offensive and defensive resources of the Alliance will be drawn upon. Such was the case in April 1980 when, for three days, 11 Group was subjected to repeated attacks by aircraft from the United States, German, Canadian, Netherlands, Norwegian, Belgian and French Air Forces. The Lightnings and Phantoms of the seven fighter squadrons were supplemented as they would be in actual conflict above, by the Lightnings of the Lightning Training Flight at Binbrook, the Phantoms of No 228 OCU at Coningsby and the Hawks and Hunters from the 11 Group Tactical Weapons Units at Brawdy and Lossiemouth. Alliance solidarity was confirmed by the commitment to the defence of the United Kingdom by USAF F-15s and F-5s which reflected their likely wartime roles. Altogether, some 100 aircraft defended United Kingdom airspace against 300 aggressors. On the ground, air bases were defended by the RAF Regiment against 'diversionary brigades' or 'saboteurs', the Royal Observer Corps was deployed and Bloodhound and Rapier units were exercised.

Royal Air Force Wattisham was opened to the national press for the third day of the exercise, which began with a low-level attack by six Luftwaffe F-4K Phantoms, followed quickly by four F-104 Starfighters of the Royal Canadian Air Force. Synchronised with the attacks, ground explosions were detonated and the passive defence units of the station had to cope with fires and 'casualties' while full operational response was being maintained by the squadrons. A more sinister attack was made by a lone aggressor Hunter which, in a single highspeed low-level pass, simulated a chemical attack but, thoroughly drilled in many station exercises, all ground personnel had already donned their nuclear biological and chemical dress and still the Phantoms of 56

and 23 Squadrons continued to get airborne. Finally, by the end of one 36-hour period the two squadrons alone had made almost 200 interceptions. As Air Vice Marshal Peter Latham, AOC 11 Group observed, 'Most excellent. Britain's air defence is the very best we can do with our resources. We have a highly skilled force with very good equipment.'

The Future

The offensive capability, however, of the Warsaw Pact Air Forces continues to grow. So, in addition to the improvements in hand for the ground environment of the UK Air Defence, the other equipment in the active defence must also be progressively strengthened. At the centre of the re-equipment programme is the Panavia Tornado F Mk 2: the Air Defence Variant of the international multi-role combat aircraft already entering RAF service in its interdictor strike (IDS) role. 165 Tornado F2s will ultimately replace all the Royal Air Force's Phantoms and Lightnings both in the United Kingdom and in Royal Air Force Germany. Full-scale development of the F2 was authorised by the British government in March 1976, and by the end of 1980 three prototypes were flying. It is scheduled to enter service in 1984.

A reminder of the likely air defence operational environment in the next generation serves to emphasise just how important the F-2 will be. The United Kingdom could be threatened from many directions by large numbers of enemy aircraft in a short space of time. They could seek to penetrate at low or medium level, at high or supersonic speeds and could carry free-fall or stand-off weapons. They would very likely be accompanied by comprehensive electronic countermeasure (ECM) support. Moreover, a proportion might get through to damage our airfields.

Tornado F2 Air Defence Variant

Designed to meet the RAF's commitment for air defence of the extensive UK Air Defence Region, the Tornado F2 has a long range autonomous capability which will enable operations some 350nm from base in bad weather, in heavy ECM and against multiple targets at high or low level. With tanker support the Tornado F2 is designed to have a loiter time of several hours.

Above: Tornado F2 on trials over the Irish Sea.

Left: Carrying a mixed load of ordnance during trials: Skyshadow ECM pods on wingtip pylons; on inner pylons subsonic fuel tanks and AIM-9 SRAAMs; under fuselage Kormoran anti-shipping missiles.

Right: During air defence trials, a Tornado F2 with a combat air patrol weapons fit of four Sky Flash rockets semi-recessed under the fuselage, two AIM-9L Sidewinders and long range fuel tanks on wing pylons. The variable geometry wings (fully spread span 13.90m, fully swept 8.60m) are here in the forward sweep position used for take-off, landing and subsonic 'loitering'. On detecting enemy aircraft the Tornado sweeps its wings and accelerates to supersonic speeds to identify and, if necessary, engage the intruders with its Sky Flash missiles.

The F2 will, therefore, be called upon to operate for extended periods on combat patrols over an area stretching from the North Eastern Atlantic, across the North Sea to the mouth of the Baltic, down to the English Channel and, in addition, to contribute towards the air defence of the Central Region of Europe. In those areas, it will not only be protecting approaches to the United Kingdom, but covering Allied maritime forces below it. Finally, it must be able to get airborne from damaged runways.

The production model F2 will be powered by uprated RB199-34R-04 turbo-fan engines at present installed in the IDS Tornado. Each possesses about 8,000lb static thrust raised to 15,000lb with reheat. Its fuselage is slightly larger than the IDS to accommodate the nose radome and four Sky Flash missiles. However, the extension has provided additional space for avionics and fuel as well as permitting further improvements to aerodynamic performance. Its basic operational radius of 400 miles will be extended by in-flight refuelling and its supersonic acceleration will be superior to that of the IDS.

As well as the four Sky Flash air-to-air guided missiles, F2 will carry four Raytheon AIM-9L Sidewinders on underwing pylons and a Mauser 27mm cannon recessed in the starboard fuselage. An integral part of the complete weapon system is the new Marconi airborne interceptor radar named Foxhunter. The radar operates in the 3cm Ib band and uses pulse doppler techniques described by Marconi as Frequency Modulated Intermittent Continuous Wave. It carries a wide range of electronic countermeasure features and can track a number of targets simultaneously at a detection range in excess of 100 miles. The Sky Flash missile, itself, will be able to engage targets at a distance of 25 miles at very low level and can both discriminate between closely bunched targets and isolate them from background earth clutter.

Tactical implications of the F2's advanced equipment are considerable. The integration of the aircraft's weapons management and information display systems will permit the crew to respond to directions from the airborne early warning aircraft or the ground without speech transmissions and, because of their full awareness of their immediate tactical environment, to act independently of any external control if circumstances should demand it. As long as external communications do remain open, the aircraft will be able to receive real-time information on unidentified aircraft and jamming sources which will permit the swiftest and most economic allocation of fighter resources where they are most needed. Thus, the highest degree of centralised guidance may be safely and simply co-ordinated with a considerable amount of autonomous operation.

The ability to identify enemy aircraft in time to derive the greatest benefit from the weapons systems will be helped not just by the data links with other units in the defence organisation, but by equipment carried by the F2 itself. The IFF interrogator will be valuable, but like any other IFF system will be vulnerable to spoofing and other electronic countermeasures in war. Until ECM resistant equipment is designed, further reliance will be placed on a visual augmentation system which is a low light TV camera to allow clear air identification by day and night. In addition, the Radar Homing and Warning Receiver is primarily designed to give the crew visual and audio warning of imminent threats. This equipment, however, will obviously assist identification by distinguishing between signals emitted by hostile and friendly radars.

The final advantage, shared by F2 with the GR1, is its ability to operate with full weapon and fuel load from less than 1,000yd of concrete. With its integral auxiliary power unit and on-board unserviceability identification and diagnosis systems and secure comprehensive communications net, F2 can be dispersed well away from its home base provided it has access to fuel, weapons and groundcrew. Indeed, the advent of F2 into 11 Group will present a challenge to the imagination of her operators to ensure that the aircraft's enormous potential is fully realised.

In time of tension another, less spectacular but very effective dispersal would take place to strengthen the United Kingdom's air defences. The decision was made in 1979 to modify 85 Hawk training aircraft to carry the AIM-9L Sidewinder. The Hawk is a small single-engined multi-purpose transonic trainer whose primary role at RAF Chivenor and RAF Brawdy is to convert fast jet pilots from basic flying training to their ultimate operational

AIR DEFENCE OF THE UNITED KINGDOM IN THE 1980s

Sector Operations Centre

1 At several hundred miles from coastline a Nimrod AEW aircraft identifies incoming raid of Backfires.
2 Information transmitted to network of operations centres for command decisions.

16

tasks. It has a maximum speed of Mach 0.88 in level flight and Mach 1.2 in a shallow dive and it can carry up to 6,500lb of weapons including Sidewinders. Although restricted to clear air operations, when dispersed to airfields throughout the United Kingdom, the highly manoeuvrable Hawk will provide a valuable short-range addition to local air defences and will obviously complicate the task of any enemy aircraft which might penetrate the Tornado screen.

In the longer term, just as the AIM-9L has replaced earlier Marks of Sidewinder, so Sky Flash will be replaced by a new international collaborative radar-guided medium range air-to-air weapon, and Sidewinder itself by a short range heat-seeking weapon. It is envisaged that the North Atlantic Treaty Alliance will collaborate on procuring both weapons, with the United States taking the lead in the longer range equipment and a European consortium, including the United Kingdom, being responsible for the infra-red weapon. By the 1990s, it can be expected that the medium range missile will have a reliable IFF interrogator, a low vulnerability to ECM by deception or Jamming and will be able to destroy small low flying targets at considerable range. The short range weapon is likely to be extremely agile, resistent to flare deception and because of its sensitivity to temperature variation, able to attack an aircraft from any angle.

Airborne Early Warning

But, however good the fighter aircraft and however deadly their weapons, enemy intruders are not only likely to have the advantage of tactical surprise, but they will have a lot of airspace in which to seek concealment. Consequently, the entry into service in 1982 of the Nimrod Airborne Early Warning aircraft to replace the venerable Shackleton will be of enormous significance to the United Kingdom air defence. The British Government had originally intended to join with NATO in an Alliance purchase of a number of United States E-3 Sentry Airborne Warning and Control (AWAC) aircraft but lengthy delays in the ability of the Allies to agree the conditions of such a purchase led to the British decision in March 1977 to develop the Nimrod airframe and engines as a national AEW aircraft. It was believed that any further delay in preparing the replacement for the Shackleton would leave a serious gap in the United Kingdom air defence system. The first Service Nimrod AEW is expected to reach its designated base at Waddington in 1982 with the squadron numbers completed by 1985.

It is readily distinguishable from its maritime predecessors by the bulbous radomes mounted on the nose and tail. In wing-tip pods it carries electronic support measures equipment. Not surprisingly, Nimrod AEW has been described as 'a flying radar station'. Two Ferranti FIN-1012 inertial navigation platforms

provide the information about the aircraft's own position, heading and attitude which must be absolutely accurate so that the rest of the system may be reliable. Its function is to complement ground-based radars by extending coverage much further away from the United Kingdom's coastline and to much lower levels. Nimrod will provide early warning information to the air defence network and should ground control units be eliminated from the conflict, it could control fighters directly itself. Unlike AWACS, however, it is not designed to provide an alternative airborne control post for offensive operations.

The aircraft will use three methods to detect and clarify targets. First, is the pulse doppler radar which operates in two modes: high pulse repetition frequency for tracking fast moving targets and a lower range which would identify slow moving objects such as ships. The radar's extensive electronic counter countermeasures protection will be enhanced by frequency agility. The second method of detection is the IFF Interrogator which is co-ordinated with the radar response reception and the third, the electronic support measure equipment which automatically compares emissions received with those stored in its memory bank. Communication with other elements in the air defence ground environment, AWACS and Royal Navy ships will initially be by NATO data link 11 and, subsequently, by the spectrum, highly secure joint tactical information distribution system (JTIDS). The advent of Nimrod AEW will therefore make undetected low level intrusion of UK airspace a very difficult proposition for many years ahead.

The New Team

In addition, the ability of Tornado to take advantage of the longer range activities of Nimrod AEW will be further enhanced by expansion of the RAF's in-flight refuelling fleet described fully in Chapter 4. To the 23 Victor K Mk 2s will be added the nine VC-10s purchased in 1978 and due to enter service at Brize Norton between 1982 and 1983.

Defence policy decisions of the 1950s which alleged that there would be little further threat to the United Kingdom from the manned bomber, and that consequently there was no need to build an interceptor successor to the Lightning have been proved by the Warsaw Pact Air Forces to be premature. It was, however, much easier to run defences down than to reconstruct them and it is only in the 1980s that the country can look to a major strengthening of all aspects of United Kingdom air defence with the advent of Tornado F2, new weapons, a new ground environment, the Nimrod AEW, the VC-10 tankers and steadily increasing surface-to-air missile defences. It will not be forgotten that all other military operations must depend in the last resort on the security of the home base which is the ultimate responsibility of the air defence system of the United Kingdom.

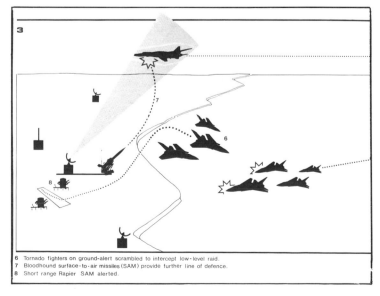

Tornado F2 aircraft commanded to intercept with Sky Flash missile.
Other Tornados standing by (with VC10 tanker providing in-flight refuelling) on combat air patrol.
Low-level incoming raid of Fencers identified by coastal radars.

6 Tornado fighters on ground-alert scrambled to intercept low-level raid.
7 Bloodhound surface-to-air missiles (SAM) provide further line of defence.
8 Short range Rapier SAM alerted.

Phantom

The Rolls-Royce Spey-powered Phantom is at the moment the standard RAF air defence fighter in Strike Command but will be replaced in the 1980s with the Tornado. Two main variants are used, the FG1 which was originally designed as a naval interceptor but entered service with the RAF in 1968, and the FGR2 which also entered service in 1968 and was used until 1974 in the strike/attack and reconnaissance roles. Both types are armed with a 20mm six-barrelled Vulcan gun, Sparrow and Sidewinder air-to-air missiles and both have a Mach 2 capability.

Above left: An FG1 of No 43 Squadron is backed into the Quick Readiness Alert hangar at Leuchars to join its partner on immediate standby for scrambling to intercept intruders.

Left: FGR2s of No 56 Squadron from Wattisham sweep low over the Ballistic Early Warning System at Fylingdales in North Yorkshire.

Above: FGR2 of No 56 Squadron on the tarmac at Wattisham.

Centre right: FGR2 of No 111 Squadron displays its hardware — four Sparrow radar-homing missiles on fuselage pylons and four Sidewinders outboard.

Bottom right: FG1 of No 43 Squadron climbing away from Leuchars in reheat.

Fighter Control

The eyes and ears of the air defence of the UK are the unobtrusive team of Fighter Controllers who spot intruders at long range and direct the fighters towards interception.

Right: Controllers at their consoles.

Below: Air Traffic Control at Wattisham with No 56 Squadron on the tarmac.

Ground Support

Similarly indispensible to the successful execution of the air defence mission are the groundcrew who have to maintain armed aircraft ready for immediate take-off and interception.

Above: Rearming the Gatling gunpod for a Phantom GR2 of No 29 Squadron at Coningsby.

Left: First-line servicing for a Phantom at Coningsby.

Right: A Canberra of No 100 Squadron at RAF Marham, Norfolk is prepared for another gunnery practice sortie for Lightnings and Phantoms over the North Sea.

Lightning

Powered by two vertically-stacked Rolls-Royce Avon engines, the Lightning has been in RAF service since the 1960s. Destined to be replaced by the Tornado F2, it is still a potent Mach 2 interceptor whose weapons' fit includes the Red Top infra-red guided AAM.

Right: Representatives of the Lightning Wing from Binbrook over the North Sea. A T5 from the Lightning Training Flight leads F6s from No 5 Squadron (port) and No 11 Squadron.

Below: Lightning F6 of No 5 Squadron on the tarmac at Binbrook.

Airborne Early Warning

Above: Due to enter service in 1982, the Nimrod AEW3 can provide at long range and at low or high altitude, detection, tracking and classification of aircraft, missiles and ships; interceptor control, direction of strike aircraft, air defence, air traffic control and SAR facilities.

Left: Mockup of the controllers' console to be fitted in the Nimrod AEW variant.

Above: Shackleton AEW2 of No 8 Squadron, due to be replaced by the Nimrod AEW3. The Shackleton MR1 first entered RAF service in 1951 but was given a new lease of life in 1971 as a long range maritime reconnaissance and early warning aircraft. For this purpose all armament was removed and a range of new equipment was added including AN/APS-20 (F)1 search radar transferred from retired Gannet AEW3s which was placed in a radome under the forward fuselage. With a crew of 12, the Shackleton AEW2 can remain on station for up to 10 hours.

Right: Closeup of Shackleton AEW2 'Juliet' of No 8 Squadron on standby at Lossiemouth in 1981, giving a good view of the radome.

24

3

Strike and Attack

Since the days of Lord Trenchard it has been well realised in the Royal Air Force that a good defence may deny a victory to the opponent, but to defeat him requires a successful counter offensive. In World War 2, Bomber Command launched 235,319 sorties against Germany, dropping 657,674 tons of bombs on industrial and military targets. As a result, not only was German war production finally crippled, but more and more of her war resources were diverted to air defence: aircraft, radars, anti-aircraft weapons and anti-aircraft troops. So much so, that by 1943 Germany was forced to produce more shells for anti-aircraft guns than for anti-tank weapons even though she was at the time desperately trying to hold the massive Russian armoured counter offensives. In addition, in all theatres of war where British troops were engaged on the ground, tactical aircraft harassed enemy forces, destroyed his reinforcement routes, dislocated the resources moving along them and generally added the enormous speed and impact of airpower to the traditional land battle. By 1981, the RAF could deliver more destructive force upon an enemy in one set of sorties than was carried in the whole of World War 2. The responsibilities for that attacking strength were shared between the squadrons of No 1 Group of RAF Strike Command, the offensive squadrons of No 38 Group and the squadrons of RAF Germany which are described in Chapter 6.

The Vulcan Force

The direct heirs to the traditions of Bomber Command are the six squadrons of Vulcan B Mk 2s of No 1 Group based at RAF Scampton and RAF Waddington in Lincolnshire. First flown on 30 August 1952, the Vulcan entered service in February 1957 with No 230 OCU, now at Scampton but then down the road at Waddington. Five months later, 83 Squadron became operational with the Vulcan B1 also at Waddington. For 11 years the Vulcans were the mainstay of the British nuclear deterrent force until the Royal Navy's Polaris submarine fleet assumed the responsibility in mid-1969.

In those 11 years, although the role remained the same, operational circumstances and equipment were considerably modified. The Vulcan had been designed in the late 1940s as a

Below: Vulcan B2 of No 27 Squadron over the North Sea.

high speed, high level bomber. That operational concept was challenged in 1960 when a Soviet SAM brought down Gary Powers' U-2 from a height well in excess of 70,000ft. The fact that it had taken 13 SAMs to knock down the lightweight reconnaissance aircraft and that one had also destroyed a MiG fighter which was vainly trying to intercept, were not known at the time but even had they been, it soon became clear that the upper airspace no longer afforded a guaranteed sanctuary to a high speed bomber. Moreover, as Soviet surface-to-air defences began to extend across Eastern Europe and Western Russia, it became necessary for the RAF to revise the overall concepts of offensive operations. Whereas the United States Air Force came to develop medium level operations with large scale defence suppression, the RAF elected to rely primarily on high speed, low level intrusion to press home offensive sorties.

In 1960, the Vulcan B2 began to enter service, with increased wingspan, four Bristol Siddeley Olympus engines and greatly improved electronic equipment. In 1966, the entire force switched from high to low level operations thereby extending its operational effectiveness by many years even in the face of extended surface-to-air defences. After the nuclear deterrent responsibility had been transferred to the Navy, the Vulcan Force was assigned to SACEUR. Twenty years after entering service, the B2 remained a formidable weapon system: able to carry either 21,000lb of conventional bombs or tactical nuclear weapons at low level by day or by night in all weathers, deep into the territory of the Warsaw Pact, against troop concentrations, communications, airfields and other major military targets. The presence of such a force meant that no Warsaw Pact commander could ever be certain that his offensive could proceed without dislocation or disruption or that reinforcements could be presumed immune from air attack in bad weather and darkness. Moreover, should ever nuclear weapons be required to respond to Warsaw Pact aggression, the Vulcans would add the flexibility of the long range manned aircraft to SACEUR's tactical nuclear weapons arsenal.

The Squadrons

All six Vulcan B2 Squadrons have long bomber traditions. At Waddington, No 9 was the first RFC Squadron to be equipped with radio in 1914 and since then, with the exception of a few months at the end of World War 1, has remained a bomber squadron. It took part in the raid against the experimental rocket station at Peenemunde and with 617 Squadron its Lancasters attacked and sank the German battleship *Tirpitz* at Tromso in 1944. Flight Sergeant George Thompson, a wireless operator with No 9 Squadron, on a daylight raid in January 1945 earned one of Bomber Command's 23 Victoria Crosses while saving the lives of two fellow crew members in his burning aircraft. Later, the squadron's Canberras took part in the Suez operation in 1956. Since 1962, it has flown the Vulcan B2.

No 44 was originally formed as a night fighter squadron in 1917 but since 1937 has flown bombers, being first to receive the Lancaster at Waddington in December 1941. In April 1942, Squadron Leader J. V. Nettleton won the VC for leading a low level daylight raid against Augsburg in the face of very heavy defences. No 44 also took part in the Suez operations. It has flown Vulcans from Waddington since August 1960.

No 50 Squadron also began service as a fighter unit in the defence of the United Kingdom in World War 1, but fought throughout World War 2 with Hampdens, Manchesters and Lancasters as part of the Bomber Command main force from airfields in the Lincoln area. Squadron members won one VC, six DSOs, 70 DFCs and 114 DFMs. It has flown Vulcans from Waddington since 1961.

No 101, the fourth Waddington squadron, has been a bomber unit since its formation at Farnborough in 1917. Its Blenheims attacked German invasion barges in the Channel ports in 1940 and later its Lancasters contributed to the radio counter-measures war, carrying equipment to jam Luftwaffe night-fighter

frequencies. In May 1951, No 101 became the first RAF Squadron to re-equip with Canberras and took part in anti-terrorist operations in Malaya. It has flown Vulcans since 1958.

On the other side of Lincoln at Scampton, No 230 OCU trains the five-man crews for the Vulcan fleet. A small number will stay on the base for duty with 27 Squadron, flying the Vulcan SR2 which inherited the RAF's strategic reconnaissance role from the Victors of 543 Squadron in 1974. A slightly 'different' role is not new for No 27 because since its formation in 1915 it has discharged reconnaissance, bombing, imperial policing, training, fighter, anti-shipping, ground attack (when its commanding officer, Wing Commander J. B. Nicholson won the VC), jungle rescue, transport during the Berlin Airlift, attack at Suez and Blue Steel responsibilities during the period of the deterrent force. It now contributes to the RAF's maritime and strategic reconnaissance operations.

No 35 Squadron also spent some time as a general purpose unit until 1929, since when it has flown most of the bombers which have seen RAF service. It was the first squadron to receive the Halifax in 1940 and became a founder member of the Pathfinder Force in August 1942. The squadron honours include 19 DSOs, six Bars to the DSO, one MC, 295 DFCs, 27 Bars to the DFC, four CGMs, 173 DFMs, and two Bars to the DFM. It has flown the Vulcan B2 since 1963.

The third Scampton squadron is the youngest but perhaps the best known. No 617 was formed at Scampton in March 1943 with the express purpose of attacking the Ede, Mohne and Sorpe Dams in the heart of the German industrial Ruhr. After the legendary, successful raid of 16 May it remained in service as a specialist low-level unit as well as contributing to main bombing and pathfinding duties in No 5 Group including raids with 12,000lb and 22,000lb bombs on V-weapon bases and on the *Tirpitz*. It was only the second RAF squadron to produce two VCs: Wing Commander Guy Gibson for the Dams raid and Wing Commander Leonard Cheshire for his consistent leadership on every mission no matter how hazardous or difficult and for pioneering very low level target marking. It has flown Vulcans from Scampton since 1958 and in June 1961 a Vulcan B1A of No 617, captained by Squadron Leader M. G. Beavis, established a new world record for a flight between England and Australia in 20 hours, three minutes. No 617 will be the first RAF squadron to re-equip with the Tornado GR1 in 1982.

The Buccaneer

The other long range offensive aircraft in No 1 Group are the Buccaneers from RAF Lossiemouth. The majority are assigned to SACLANT for maritime duties, as explained in Chapter 4, but No 208, which has flown the Buccaneer S2A since 1974 is employed in the overland deep interdiction or counter-air roles. Originally designed for anti-shipping operations for the Royal Navy, the Buccaneer was bought for the RAF after the cancellation of TSR-2 and the decision not to buy the F-111 from the USA. It has since proved an excellent low level weapon platform and No 208, like the Vulcan Force, is assigned to SACEUR for wartime use.

The aircraft can carry a wide range of conventional and nuclear weapons in its capacious bomb-bay and has been flown on trials both for laser-guided bombs and for the flight trials of the Tornado weapon management systems. It may be equipped with the anti-radar version of the stand-off Martel anti-radiation missile and the Westinghouse AN/ALQ-101 electronic counter-measures pod to facilitate low level penetration through heavy surface-to-air defences. Hostile interceptors will be inhibited by the Sidewinder missiles which it can carry in addition to its offensive weapon load. Like the Vulcan, the Buccaneer will in due course be replaced by the Tornado GR1.

Air-to-Air Refuelling

Buccaneers can also be used to refuel their colleagues in flight, but

more normally such assistance is provided by the two specialist Victor squadrons from Marham. The Victor was the third RAF V-bomber to enter RAF service at No 232 OCU at Gaydon in 1957. After serving as a bomber with various squadrons and in the strategic reconnaissance role with No 543 Squadron, the B Mk 2 was modified in 1965 to the air-to-air refuelling (AAR) role. It carries a total of 128,000lb of fuel which theoretically is all transferable. It can itself be refuelled in flight by other Victors. Its four Rolls-Royce Conway RCo17 Mk 201 turbo-jets generate 80,000lb of static thrust and provide a maximum range in excess of 4,000 miles. In recent years, as explained in Chapter 2, a large proportion of AAR is dedicated to the air defence of the United Kingdom and of Royal Naval vessels in home waters. Nevertheless, although withdrawal from many overseas commitments has reduced the demand for long range 'strategic' refuelling there are regular demands from fighters deploying to Sardinia or Cyprus or further afield from Harriers en route to Belize or Buccaneers and Jaguars crossing the Atlantic to participate in the Red Flag exercises in Nevada. The 23 Victors are apportioned at Marham to No 232 OCU, to Nos 55 and 57 Squadrons and to a reserve. No 55 Squadron was one of the oldest specialist bomber squadrons before converting to the AAR role in 1965. It was a unit in the 41st Wing of the Royal Flying Corps, the forerunner of the Independent Bombing Force which itself was a progenitor of the concepts and objectives of Bomber Command in World War 2. Between 1939 and 1945, No 55 Squadron operated mainly in the Middle East, flying 352 sorties for example in the first ten days of the Battle of Alamein. It has flown various Marks of Victors since 1960. No 57 Squadron was also a long range bomber squadron in World War 1 and in World War 2 operated from bases in France against the advancing German armies in May 1940. It subsequently flew Wellingtons and Lancasters against a wide variety of targets in Germany and in support of allied troops in 1944 and 1945. It has flown Victors since 1959 and AAR K Mk 2s from Marham since 1967.

Offensive Support

Although in World War 2 heavy bombers such as those from 57 Squadron provided support to the invading forces, shorter range offensive operations were primarily the responsibility of the ground attack squadrons. In 1980, shorter range offensive operations from squadrons based in the United Kingdom are the responsibility of the Jaguars and Harriers of No 38 Group. At Coltishall, Nos 6 and 54 fly the Anglo-French Jaguar GR1 in the close support and battlefield interdiction roles. Unlike their colleagues at Bruggen they are equipped only with conventional weapons. The comprehensive development of surface-to-air defences not only forced attack aircraft to make the greatest use of low level cover, they put a premium on swift target acquisition, precise weapon aiming and preferably a single pass attack. The computerised navigation and weapon attack equipment, laser range finder and other modern systems described in detail in Chapter 6 are specifically designed to maximise the Jaguar's effectiveness in complex low level combat. The Jaguar pilot workload is demanding and it is no coincidence that Nos 6 and 54 Squadrons have long and proud traditions. No 6 has been associated with close air support for the greater part of its history since forming at Farnborough in January 1914. From 1919 to 1969, it saw unbroken service in the Middle East, quelling insurgency in Iraq, peace-keeping in Palestine, and mounting ground attack sweeps in the Western Desert against the Italians and Rommel's Afrika Korps. Subsequently, the Squadron flew Spitfires, Venoms and Canberras until 1969 when it disbanded for the first time in 55 years. Later that year, it reformed in the United Kingdom at Coningsby with Phantoms in the ground attack and tactical reconnaissance roles before converting to the Jaguar GR1 in 1974.

No 54, on the other hand, has a long tradition of a fighter squadron since its formation at Castle Bromwich in World War 1. In World War 2 it was heavily involved in the Battle of Britain flying Spitfires from Hornchurch. Among its distinguished pilots were Pilot Officer C. F. Gray who shot down 16 enemy aircraft, Flying Officer D. A. P. McMullen who shot down 13, and Flight Lieutenant (later Air Commodore) Al Deere. After 1945 it was successively equipped with Vampires, Meteors and Hunters until in March 1960 it received Hunter FGA9s and began to specialise in ground attack operations. It also received Jaguar GR1s in 1974.

The third Jaguar Squadron at Coltishall, No 41, also has a fighter tradition. Formed at Gosport in 1916 the Squadron has served almost entirely in the United Kingdom. It was also heavily engaged in the Battle of Britain relieving No 54 at Hornchurch at the beginning of September. Pilot Officer E. S. Lock, with 17 kills, was one of the highest serving pilots of the Battle. Its modern role, however, is slightly different in that, like No 2 Squadron at Laarbruch, it provides the tactical reconnaissance essential in a fast-moving air and land campaign.

Unlike the squadrons in RAF Germany, however, the three Jaguar units at Coltishall would not necessarily operate in the Central Region of Europe. They are assigned to SACEUR's Strategic Reserve (Air) which is a force of RAF and USAF squadrons normally based in the United Kingdom which could redeploy at short notice to airfields anywhere on the mainland of Europe to strengthen defences or to reinforce air attacks on enemy armour and airfields. Consequently, also unlike their colleagues in Germany, these crews are trained in air-to-air refuelling. One of the Jaguar Squadrons has an alternative operational role as part of the air element of the United Kingdom Mobile Force, a self-supporting air and land force equipped to counter armour and mechanised infantry and trained for operations in each area of Allied Command Europe. A further mobile force, with a more restricted strategic role, is the Allied Command Europe Mobile Force (AMF) which is a multi-national land and air force which could rapidly deploy to either the northern or southern flanks of the Alliance. Its function is primarily to demonstrate promptly the collective resolve of the Alliance rather than to provide extensive defence in depth.

Great emphasis is placed on Arctic warfare and the fourth offensive support squadron in No 38 Group, No 1, is an important element in the force. Flying Harrier GR3s from its base at Wittering, No 1 Squadron is also assigned to SACEUR's Strategic Reserve (Air). Like the Jaguar, Harrier can operate from short, damaged or makeshift runways but its STOVL or VTOL quality makes it especially valuable to operations from remote sites out on NATO's flanks. While its deployment options cover a much wider area, its operational methods and equipment resemble those of the Harrier Wing at Gutersloh. It is particularly appropriate that No 1 should, in 1980, operate closely with ground forces because it was formed in 1912 from the balloons, airships and kites of No 1 Airship Company of the Air Battalion of the Royal Engineers. Since then, it has won battle honours on the Western Front in World War 1, the North-West Frontier of India, Iraq, France in 1939/40, the Battle of Britain, where the squadron flew Hurricanes from Tangmere and Northolt throughout the Battle and, finally, as a long-range escort squadron to daylight bombing raids against Germany. In July 1969 it became the first operational squadron in the world to fly vertical take-off fighters and pioneered offensive support to ground forces from dispersed sites close to the potential battlefield.

The Re-equipment Programme

Thus, in 1981, the offensive strike and attack power of the RAF remained formidable, but many aircraft had seen several years' service and the defences against which they would be called upon to fly were becoming progressively more complex. It was, therefore, timely that a major re-equipment programme was under way which would transform both the deep strike/attack and offensive support capabilities by a new generation of aircraft, weapons and supporting equipment.

Tornado

At the centre of the RAF's re-equipment programme in the 1980s and 1990s is the PANAVIA Tornado: the product of allied collaboration by the British Aerospace Corporation, Messerschmitt-Boelkow-Blohm and Aer Italia. By 1981 its flight trials were well advanced and the quantum jump in technology over previous European design combat aircraft was very plain to see.

The twin Turbo Union RB-199s have the highest thrust-to-volume ratio of any turbine engine in the world. They also have a low specific fuel consumption but for short take-off and combat manoeuvres a high reheat thrust is available. Yet, with the aid of thrust reverser, Tornado can be landed on less than 500 yards of runway, an extremely important operational consideration for future European conflict. Both attack (GR1) and interceptor (F2) versions have variable sweep wings, but those on the GR1 are swept manually back to 67°, whereas the F2 has autosweep. Consequently, at high speed and low altitudes high wing loading is possible giving a very smooth ride at Mach 0.9 at 200ft which reduces crew fatigue and enhances instrument monitoring, thereby greatly improving the overall effectiveness of the weapon platform. Handling benefits from the triplex electrical flying controls and automatic stabilisation. The Command and Stability Augmentation System (CSAS) automatically compensates for configuration changes during flight and several pilot reports have testified to the aircraft's high stability in turbulent air conditions. Maximum speed is in excess of Mach 2 in level flight.

Navigation to the target is also highly automated. The auto-pilot can follow a flight plan automatically or it can be updated by the navigator in the back seat as he monitors a combined map and radar and TV displays and makes radar or laser position fixes. The terrain-following radar is considerably more advanced than that on the F-111 and can, by integration with the CSAS, guide the aircraft at high speed at a predetermined height above the ground. Thus, maximum advantage may be taken of contours to evade detection by enemy radar.

Tornado can lift up to 16,000lb of weapons, rather more than the regular Lancaster bombload, on three under fuselage and four underwing pylons. But, more importantly, it can deliver them with much greater accuracy. Automatic computerised radar target identification can be monitored by a head-up display and followed

Left: British and German Tornados at the Cottesmore-based Tri-National Tornado Training Establishment.

Right: The first AV-8B Harrier II. Manufactured by the McDonnell Douglas Corporation with British Aerospace as a major subcontractor and Rolls-Royce supplying the Pegasus engine, the AV-8B is designed as a replacement for the existing Harrier. To be designated GR5 in British service, the RAF have indicated a requirement for 60 AV-8Bs while the USMC require 336.

by automatic procedures to weapon release point. The final precision is achieved by laser range finder but at any time the pilot may modify the attack profile or select a completely new target.

The combination of these qualities in Tornado has produced an aircraft which can deliver a large conventional or nuclear weapon load with great accuracy in all weathers by day or by night. In any future conflict an enemy cannot be expected to cease fire at dusk or in bad weather and Tornado's 24-hour availability will be indispensable to NATO. Its very low level high speed penetration, 800kts at 200ft, together with automatic radar warning and jamming equipment, a chaff dispenser and counter-measures to infra-red missiles, will reduce its vulnerability and thereby increase its availability and effectiveness. Its potential recalls that of the World War 2 Mosquito whose relative invulnerability greatly increased its 'cost-effectiveness' also. Finally, Tornado's ability to operate from damaged runways and other surfaces will reduce its vulnerability on the ground.

Meanwhile, weapons to match the airframe are under development. It can, of course, deliver the current range of free-fall and guided weapons but will be armed in the anti-airfield role with the Hunting Engineering JP-233 which is an area weapon which distributes both concrete penetrator and anti-personnel warheads which will seriously disrupt operations on any target airfield. Meanwhile, studies continue into guided anti-armour and anti-radiation weapons to replace BL-755 and Martel. Such is the potential of the Tornado airframe that it is not too fanciful to look further ahead to air-delivered stand-off weapons with different kinds of specialist sub-munition warheads with unmatched precision and lethality. In the longer term, air-launched cruise missiles may extend Tornado's range even further.

The first Tornados to enter operational service arrived at the Tri-National Tornado Training Establishment (TTTE) in July 1980. 220 GR1s and 165 F2s are expected to enter RAF service. The training establishment will have a full complement of 48 aircraft in five squadrons which will ultimately produce 170 operational crews each year for Britain, Germany and Italy. Initially, Tornado crews will convert from other fast jets but, ultimately, they will move directly from flying training. After 13 weeks at Cottesmore, RAF crews will move to Honington for weapons training prior to allocation to squadrons. It is expected that the first RAF Tornado GR1 squadron will be No 617 which will form at Honington during 1982. Thereafter, other squadrons will form at Marham, Laarbruch and elsewhere until the Vulcans, overland Buccaneers, reconnaissance Canberras and possibly some of the Jaguar squadrons will all be replaced by the Tornado. As the aircraft will also be flown by the German Air Force and Navy and the Italian Air Force, there will be a considerable degree of commonality and extended interoperability between the allies.

Offensive Support

As the Tornado entered service during late 1980 and early 1981, a decision by the United Kingdom Government was awaited on replacements for the Harrier and Jaguar. There was general agreement that the VTOL/STOVL qualities of the Harrier would become even more important in the next decade. Not only would STOVL permit continued forward dispersal for rapid response to calls for offensive support, but would be of inestimable value for operations from damaged airfields. The only doubts seemed to be

about which particular Harrier development would be chosen. The competitors were the Harrier GR5 designed by British Aerospace at Kingston, known as the 'big wing' Harrier and the McDonnell Douglas AV-8B which would be developed as a joint UK-US venture with advanced avionics and synthetic structures. Each had its proponents and, whichever was finally selected, the continued contribution of the 'jump jet' to British airpower was assured well into the 21st century. Jaguar replacement was more problematical. The need for an air superiority fighter had been well defined within the Alliance but attempts to embark on another tri-national collaborative venture were proving difficult in the face of different tactical requirements and timing among the three nations concerned: United Kingdom, France and Germany. Another possible replacement might be the McDonald/ Norththrop F-18 land-based variant of the USN Hornet. Alternatively, operational conceptual revision could lead to replacement of some Jaguars by Tornados or by a new British design. In the event, the AV-8B was chosen to replace the Harrier, while in the longer term Kingston would continue work on a supersonic version. A further Air Staff Target, No 410, was disclosed for a lightweight supersonic air superiority/guard attack fighter for the 1990s.

Air-to-Air Refuelling

While attention naturally focused on the dramatic impact of the Tornado's entry into service, a less spectacular but most important part of the re-equipment programme was underway. The RAF's intention to form a third air-to-air refuelling tanker squadron was announced in Parliament in 1978. By 1980, five ex-BOAC Standard VC-10s and four ex-East African Airways Super VC-10s were being restructured to tanker configuration at British Aerospace Filton Works. Like the Victor K Mk 2s which they will supplement, the VC-10s will have three refuelling points. The five Standard VC-10s will become K Mk 2 and the Supers K Mk 3. They will carry 165,000lb and 180,000lb of fuel respectively in five cylindrical tanks in the fuselage of each version. They will begin to enter service, probably at Brize Norton, during 1982 and delivery will be completed in 1983. The impact of these nine aircraft on both air defence and offensive operations will be out of all proportion to their numbers. Their presence will increase the capacity of the AAR fleet by some 50% and will be of particular value to both variants of Tornado.

The Prospects

There is no doubt that the public and government pressure will, quite rightly, continue to insist that the taxpayer gets the best possible value from some very expensive defence equipment. It is, therefore, reassuring to note the quality of the attack aircraft and weapons programme for the RAF in the 1980s. It will ensure that the offensive spirit demanded by Lord Trenchard 60 years ago will be well sustained into the next generation.

29

Far left: A B2 from RAF Waddington, where No 44 Squadron has been flying Vulcans since August 1960.

Left: That the Vulcan is still a potent strike aircraft was shown in the July 1980 Strike Command Bombing and Navigation Competition. Here representatives of the victorious crews of No 617 Squadron based at RAF Scampton, Lincs pose for the camera.

Below: A 617 Squadron B2 in the static display at the RAF Abingdon Open Day.

Vulcan

One of Strike Command's old stagers, the Hawker Siddeley Vulcan first entered RAF service in mid-1956. Following the transfer of responsibility for Britain's nuclear deterrent to the Royal Navy's Polaris submarines, the Vulcan's role was redefined primarily to low-level penetration and strike missions and they were scheduled to continue doing this until replacement by Tornado GR1s.

Buccaneer

Designed to meet a Naval requirement, the first Buccaneer flew on 30 April 1958. The RAF ordered their first Buccaneer — an S2B — in 1968 and since that date it has equipped units in Strike Command and RAF Germany. In 1980, following an accident attributed to a structural failure, the RAF Buccaneers were grounded for several months and it was announced that over one third of the 65 aircraft would need extensive repairs before returning to service. Happily they are now back in the front line and fulfilling their role as low level weapons platforms.

Left: A Buccaneer over winter countryside, carrying bombs and a Westinghouse AN/ALQ-101 ECM pod on underwing pylons.

Below left: A pair of No 208 Squadron Buccaneer S2As at low level.

Right: Ground maintenance for a No 208 Squadron Buccaneer.

Below: 208 Squadron Buccaneers.

Victor

Another of the V-Force, the Victor entered RAF
service in 1958. In 1972 the first K2 tanker
version first flew and by 1977 a total of 24 had
been delivered to the RAF to equip Nos 55 and
57 Squadrons. They are to be supplemented from
1982 onwards by a squadron of VC10 tankers.

Above: A Victor K1 of 214 Squadron, since
disbanded, refuelling Phantoms of No 29
Squadron.

Centre right: No 55 and 57 Squadron Victor K2s
from RAF Marham taking part in an air-to-air
refuelling exercise over the North Sea.

Bottom right: A No 57 Squadron Victor refuelling
a prototype Tornado over the north of England.

34

Ground maintenance for No 54 Squadron
Jaguars at Coltishall — (above left) voltage check
on Jaguar instruments; (above right) a close
inspection for the nosewheel on this Jaguar; (left)
avionics checks.

Jaguar

Development of the Anglo-French Jaguar began in 1965 and it entered RAF service in 1973, the first aircraft being delivered to the Operational Conversion Unit at RAF Lossiemouth, Scotland. In the strike/attack and reconnaissance squadrons in Strike Command and RAF Germany Jaguars replaced Phantom FGR2s. Powered by two 8,400lb Rolls-Royce/Turbomeca Adour 804 afterburning turbofans, the Jaguar can carry an impressive warload with attachments under fuselage and wings for up to 10,000lb of stores (Martel missiles, 1,000lb bombs, napalm tanks, rocket pods, reconnaissance packs, etc) as well as two 30mm Aden guns in the lower fuselage.

Above: Two-seat Jaguar T2 trainer of No 41 Squadron at RAF Coltishall.

Centre right: Jaguar of No 6 Squadron.

Bottom right: No 6 Squadron Jaguar in Denmark for Exercise 'Amber Express' in September 1981.

Tornado Interdiction/Strike Variant

In the 1980s the Tornado GR1 will become the major RAF weapons systems in the overland strike/attack reconnaissance roles replacing the Vulcan, Canberra and Buccaneer. Designed and built by Panavia GmbH set up in Munich in 1969, the MRCA — multi-role combat aircraft, as it was known — was a joint UK (British Aerospace, 42%), FRG (Messerschmitt-Bolkow-Blohm, 42%), and Italian (Aeritalia, 16%) project. With 220 interdictor/strike aircraft expected for the RAF, 324 for the German Navy and Air Force and 100 for the Italian Air Force, deliveries to the Tri-National Tornado Training Establishment (TTTE) began in summer 1980.

Below: From any angle, the power is obvious. ZA320 seen as built without markings, but with evidence on the tail assembly of an extensive electronic fit.

Left and above: Tornados at the TTTE —
formidable and photogenic by day and night,
round the clock.

Right: With inlets protected ZA320 is tested on
the Cottesmore detuner under the watchful eye of
a unit fire crew.

Above left: Preflight briefing for all three nations — British, German and Italian aircrew in the ops room.

Above: Refuelling a Tornado at Cottesmore.

Left: Interoperability — British and German flying clothing, British and German groundcrew.

Above right: Awaiting the weapons fit, ZA545 outside its hangar at the Tactical Weapons Conversion Unit; RAF Honington.

Right: Matching the weapon to its aircraft — the Hunting Engineering air-to-surface weapon JP233, designed to crater runways and then dislocate further operations by minelets, is fitted to a development Tornado in the British Aerospace hangar at Warton in 1977.

Above: An artist's impression of the havoc
caused on an enemy airfield by the submunitions
of a Tornado-launched JP233. Some will crater
the runway and taxiways while others will act as
anti-personnel mines with delayed action fuses.

Centre right: An essential element in the Tornado
OCU at Cottesmore is the Ground Servicing
School. Here, training specialists from the RAF
School of Education demonstrate the value of
video equipment for training Tornado
groundcrew.

Bottom right: Reheat and a night take-off.

Harrier

Deliveries to the RAF of this revolutionary vertical/short take-off and landing (V/STOL) strike aircraft began in 1967 and it entered full squadron service in 1969. Since that date the US Marine Corps, who had received the first of its Harriers ordered as AV-8As in 1971, have developed in conjunction with British Aerospace the more powerful AV-8B with a larger wing and increased weapons load. The original RAF Harrier was the GR1 but later an increase in engine power — by use of the 21,500lb Pegasus 103 engine — and fitting of an elongated nose containing the Ferranti Laser Ranging and Marker Target Seeker (LRMTS) led to the GR3 which is the current model to be found in RAF service. Used for offensive support — close support and battlefield interdiction roles — RAF Strike Command Harriers of 38 Group are closely involved in Arctic warfare, with No 1 Squadron assigned to SACEUR's Strategic Reserve Air. Exercise 'Anorak Express' saw Harriers of No 1 Squadron operating from Tromso, Norway in March 1980. Here (left) the aircraft is being covered up against the elements while (below) the RAF mobile catering unit from RAF Benson provides its services for the Air Lift Control Staff.

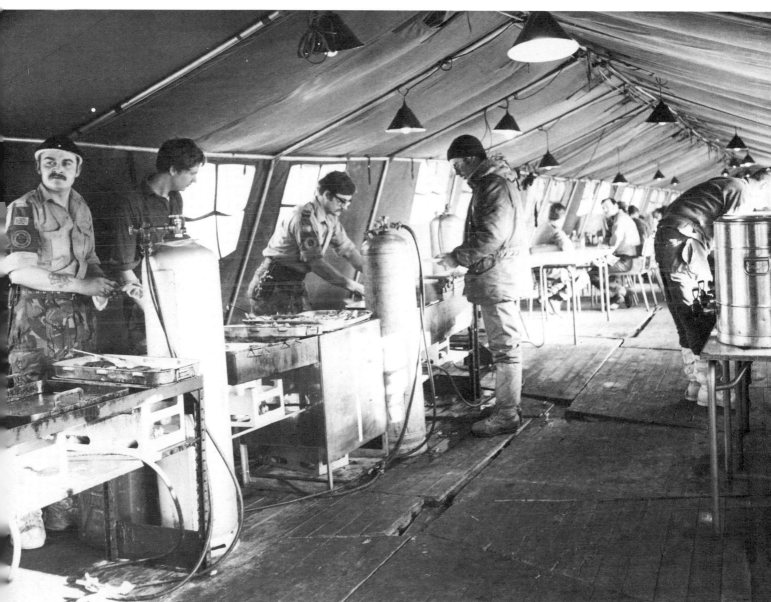

Top: A newly painted Harrier GR3 at RAF Wittering waits for its No 1 Squadron insignia to be applied.

Above: Have long range fuel tanks, will travel! The AV-8B prototype shows its ability to transit very swiftly to more distant troublespots. The latest stage in the Harrier story, the AV-8B will be known as the GR5 in RAF service and will be able to carry an impressive 9,000lb of ordnance. *McDonnell Douglas*

Right: No 1 Squadron Harrier GR3s, at low level on a sortie from RAF Wittering.

4

Maritime Operations

In her long history Britain has not only been threatened from the mainland of Europe. She has twice in this century narrowly escaped strangulation from the sea. In the indecisive Battle of Jutland in 1916 the Royal Navy failed to use its reconnaissance float planes, but since then command of the seas has ceased to be the prerogative of navies. In the 1939-45 war the U-boat was defeated when aircraft impeded its passage across the Bay of Biscay and drew the ring across the North Atlantic from North America, Iceland, the Azores and the United Kingdom. On both side battle fleets were harassed and sunk by land-based aircraft. Although by 1981 technology was far advanced on, below and above the surface of the seas the environment remained the same and there was a latent threat to the United Kingdom far greater than that posed by the German Navy of Admiral Doenitz.

The Responsibilities of No 18 Group

The major contribution of the Royal Air Force to the maritime security of the United Kingdom is made by No 18 Group of Strike Command, heir to the traditions of Coastal Command. The backbone of the Group is the Nimrod MR Mk 1 allocated to four squadrons in Scotland and Cornwall, while the Sea King helicopter is gradually replacing the Wessex and Whirlwinds of the eight Search and Rescue Flights dispersed round the United Kingdom's coastline. In common with several other Groups, however, No 18 is closely integrated within the NATO structure. AOC 18 Group at Northwood is also Air Commander Eastern Atlantic and Air Commander Channel and would, therefore, in war assume command also of the maritime patrol aircraft of Holland and Norway.

Buccaneers are tasked on tactical air support operations by Strike Command itself and air defence forces are always controlled by 11 Group.

In peacetime, maritime security also includes fishery protection and oil-rig surveillance: tasks collectively known as 'Off-Shore Tapestry'. Thus the Group flies operationally every day in peace or in war.

Maritime Reconnaissance

The work-horse of the Group is the Hawker Siddeley Nimrod (Maritime Reconnaissance) Mk 1. A unique aircraft in many respects, Nimrod is a derivative of the De Havilland Comet 4C airliner. Just as the Comet was the world's first jet airliner, so Nimrod is the world's first land-based all-jet maritime reconnaissance aircraft. Nimrod's four Rolls-Royce 250 Spey turbo-jets give it a transit cruise speed of approximately 400kts which is a considerable advantage over its piston-engine predecessors in the anti-submarine role. The modern submarine

Below: The threat — four Yakovlev Yak-36 'Forger-A' and two 'Forger-B' aircraft on the flight deck of the Soviet aircraft carrier *Kiev* taken from a Nimrod MR in July 1979.

The British Aerospace (Hawker Siddeley HS801) Nimrod MR first flew in RAF service in June 1968. Deliveries to No 201 Squadron of RAF Strike Command began on 2 October 1969 and in 1979 the first MR Mk 2 was handed over. The Nimrod MR is designed to fly at high subsonic speeds to its search area and then has a low level, low speed loiter capability (with two engines shut down) which allows a particularly long patrol endurance.

Below: Nimrod MR2 seen flying past a P&O ro-ro vessel. Note searchlight in front end of fuel pod on starboard wing leading edge.

Left: A series of photographs showing the multiple systems carried by the Nimrod MR2. (Top) The EMI Searchwater Radar Screen; (centre) The AQS 901 Sonic Receiver; (bottom) Submarine plot identified on the Tactical Display Unit.

can dive more deeply and travel more swiftly than its World War 2 ancestors and thus Nimrod's ability to reach a threatened area at high speed is very important. The anti-submarine team of surface ships, hunter killer submarines and helicopters is closely integrated, but Nimrod's contribution in searching large areas of ocean in minimum time is unique.

The Soviet Union now has more than 300 ocean-going boats: some armed with nuclear missiles, some designed to attack allied surface fleets and some designed to hunt NATO's own submarines. To detect them, Nimrod relies on a complicated blend of the human skills of a 12-man crew and advanced technology sensors. On a routine patrol from Kinloss, a Nimrod of No 120 Squadron, for example, would climb away on all four engines and transit to the search area perhaps somewhere to the North-West of the Shetlands at some 30,000ft, kept on track by the skills of the crew and an Elliot E3 inertial platform, a Decca doppler 67M and secondary Sperry GM7 Gyro Magnetic compass system. The crew would be aware of the last known position and heading of the submarine and on reaching the search area Nimrod

Right: The Soviet helicopter cruiser *Moscva* 'fixed' conclusively by Nimrod: a typical example of the unremitting long range maritime reconnaissance activities of the Nimrods of the St Mawgan and Kinloss wings.

Below: Size A Sonobuoy is lowered into the pressurised launcher; (below right) Matra Smoke Marker being fitted into the retro launcher.

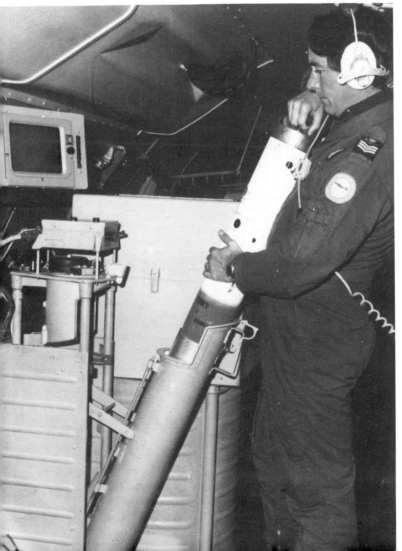

would descend to perhaps 6,000ft to begin a search pattern. The Captain would probably close down two engines. Thus with maximum fuel economy Nimrod, 'The Mighty Hunter' would begin to justify its sobriquet.

At this point, the quality of teamwork among the crew would become extremely important. Tactical information is co-ordinated and processed by the Elliot 920 computer but whereas some other maritime reconnaissance aircraft such as the P-3 Orion also rely on their tactical computer for analysis and decision-making, the Nimrod crew make the decisions based on computer information. Tactical information about the underwater intruder may be gleaned in several ways.

Occasionally, a submarine may be caught on the surface, but such an occurrence is very rare and as the Soviet Union builds more nuclear powered boats, will become rarer. Nevertheless, visual look-out remains a fundamental task. The 'Autolycus' ionisation detector was able to register diesel fumes from vessels on the surface at ranges well beyond the human vision but it is those sensors which can detect the underwater enemy which are obviously the most important. A 'Magnetic Anomaly Detector' (MAD) reacts to small changes in the earth's magnetic field caused by the presence of large amounts of metal. Electronic sensor equipment designed by Thomson-CSF of France is able to locate transmissions and bearings of electronic emissions. Nimrod's own radar may detect the tell-tale schnorkel of a submerged boat, but as often as not it will be located by the sonar buoys dropped in a meticulous pattern by the aircraft. Attached to each buoy, at a pre-set depth, is a microphone which through a small antenna protruding above the surface, transmits the sounds in the ocean back up to the Nimrod. On the central tactical display unit the attack navigator can then see the Nimrod's own track, position of the buoys and the position and heading of the boat beneath them.

Subsequent action would depend, of course, on the operating environment. In peacetime, on a routine patrol, the submarine signature, type, depth, heading and speed would be quietly logged for subsequent addition to the accumulated knowledge held by the NATO Alliance of the habits of a potential enemy. In war, however, the Nimrod's work would have only just begun. It would carry various combinations of weapons with which to destroy the submarine, or it could call up Royal Navy anti-submarine units prior to moving on itself to locating other underwater targets.

Surface Operations

Submarine hunting is not, however, Nimrod's only contribution to the maritime security of the United Kingdom. In war, it could locate, track and attack enemy surface vessels and in peacetime prepares for those activities also. For example, the Nimrod of No 120 Squadron launched from Kinloss may have located the intruding submarine after less than a couple of hours of medium level search. If so, the aircraft could still have six hours' endurance remaining. It might therefore be possible, depending on other training or operational demands, to exercise the crews' skills at surface searching. So, back up to transit height and then perhaps thirty minutes later and 180 miles to the south-west two engines closed again, let down through broken cloud to investigate a radar contact on the surface just outside British territorial waters. The Nimrod crews hope to discover a Soviet Navy Kara, Kotlin or Kresta, or even a humble intelligence gathering 'trawler' but they have been briefed before take-off on the last-known positions of such vessels and they know that their 'trade' is likely to be much more innocuous. From 6,000ft a small merchantman may be clearly visible, pitching and rolling in an averagely uncomfortable Eastern Atlantic. Down to 300ft, camera hatches open, and the Nimrod sweeps over a 5,000ton Polish coaster whose waving crew clearly see nothing sinister in the Nimrod either. Another pass, another photograph for the squadron album and, without lighting the other two engines, a steady climb and turn on to 0900 back to Kinloss. This particular sortie might be completed before dusk,

but by the very nature of its environment Nimrod must be able to operate by night and day in all weathers. Identification of surface vessels at night is made possible by a powerful 70-million candle power searchlight, the descendant of the 'Leigh' light of Bay of Biscay fame, and by an electronic flash system for night photography. The MAD, radar and sonar sensors are, of course, all applicable by night and day.

The bulk of the anti-surface shipping operations would, however, be carried out by the Buccaneers S Mk 2B of Nos 12 and 216 Squadrons and No 237 Operational Conversion Unit at Lossiemouth. No 12 has been a bomber squadron since its formation at Newhaven in 1915, flying Wellingtons and Lancasters in World War 2 and Vulcans during the zenith of the V-Force between 1962 and 1967. In 1940, Flying Officer Garland and Sergeant Gray won the first Victoria Crosses in the Royal Air Force in World War 2 when they led a low level formation attack against the heavily defended Vroenhoeven bridge over the Albert Canal in Belgium. They were both killed when their Fairey Battle was shot down but the attack was pressed home successfully. In 1969, No 12 Squadron reformed at Honington with Buccaneers and since then, being assigned to SACLANT, spends most of its training in a maritime environment. No 216 Squadron was originally a Royal Naval Air Service Bombing Unit but spent the greater part of its RAF service as a transport squadron, finally as the Royal Air Force VIP Comet Squadron from 1956 to 1975. Then, in 1979, it was reformed at Honington with aircraft from No 809 Royal Navy Squadron, disbanded after the withdrawal from service of HMS *Ark Royal*.

Below: A Martel air-to-surface guided missile, with anti-radiation warhead, on the wing pylon of a Buccaneer from RAF Honington in 1980.

The British Aerospace development Buccaneer from
Holme on Spalding Moor test flies the RAF's future
anti-shipping weapon: Sea Eagle. The Sea Eagle is an
air-launched, sea-skimming anti-ship missile for use
against warships with the most up-to-date ECM
capabilities. It is planned to enter service in the
mid-1980s.

The Buccaneer was originally designed by the Blackburn Aircraft Company for the anti-shipping role. Its two Rolls Royce-Spey bypass engines develop over 22,000lb thrust and give it extended low level range. In its large bomb-bay it can carry 1,000lb bombs or nuclear weapons, while on wing pylons it flies with rockets or the Martel TV guided stand-off missile. A typical attack profile comprises a high level 450kts approach to a point outside the radar cover of the hostile ships, then a drop to 200ft above sea level. The final attack would be made either as a singleton or in a loose formation at slightly more than wave-top height to Martel release point.

Additional reconnaissance and target information in war would continue to be given in the near future by the Vulcan SR2s of No 27 Squadron from Scampton and the Canberras of No 7 Squadron from St Mawgan. In due course, however, these specific roles will be undertaken by other sensors and both Vulcans and Canberras will be withdrawn from service.

But the Nimrod and Buccaneer forces, on the other hand, will be considerably strengthened. The conversion of the Nimrod fleet to Mk 2 standard was well under way in 1981. Outwardly similar to the Mk 1, the Mk 2 has been refitted with new sensor equipment, communications and Central Tactical Display which make it the most advanced long-range maritime patrol aircraft in the world. One of the sensor systems is the EMI Searchwater radar, which can detect and classify surface targets in high sea states at distances far greater than any other maritime radar. Information about large numbers of simultaneous targets can be swiftly transferred to the main Tactical Display Unit which has been redesigned to cater for increased navigational precision, computing speed and display quality. The new digital computer for the Central Tactical System confers a 50-fold increase in capacity over that of the Nimrod Mk 1.

Underwater detection has been improved by the installation of the AQS-901 acoustic system which analyses and provides classification data for active and passive sonar buoys of the most modern variety either in use or under development in Britain and elsewhere in the Alliance and Commonwealth. AQS-901 will display both sonar management and acoustic data thereby enabling the operator to avoid mutual interference between sonar buoys dropped in a pattern. A large numbers of buoys may be monitored simultaneously and the data preserved for post-flight analysis.

The ability of Nimrod 2 to work as a member of a team has also been enhanced. A new communication system has been fitted which includes new transmitters, a radio-teletype terminal and on-line encryption system. Finally, advanced electronic warfare equipment has been housed in new wing-pods to enhance the collection of electronic emissions. In due course, improved torpedoes and other anti-shipping weapons will increase the effectiveness of the aircraft still further.

Meanwhile, the Buccaneer's punch will be extended and strengthened by the procurement of a new sea-skimming anti-surface vessel missile, the P3T Sea Eagle. Sea Eagle will have a greater range and resistance to electronic counter-measures than the Martel and will be able to operate in all weathers by day and night. It should enter service with the Buccaneers in the mid-1980s. Thus, together with Allied navies and air forces, British maritime airpower will continue to present a formidable obstacle to any aggressor who wishes to attack by sea.

Off-Shore Tapestry

But not all the Nimrods which leave Kinloss or St Mawgan each day are training for wartime roles. Some will take off to make an immediate contribution to the security of British resources in peacetime, embarking on patrols associated with tasks known collectively in Whitehall as 'Off-Shore Tapestry': protection of fisheries, oilfields and rigs in the waters round the British coast. The Government decided in 1974 to begin regular surveillance of the oilrigs and associated fields, demonstrating by the presence of ships and aircraft its interest in a multi-million pound industry in which it had heavily invested. By the end of 1976, however, patrol of the oilfields became co-ordinated with fishery protection. In January 1977, the United Kingdom established a 200 mile Exclusive Economic Zone (EEZ) off the national coastlines. Even where the water depth is less than 600ft, that is an area of 180,000 square miles or twice that of the mainland. The Zone is divided into four patrol areas of which three are allocated to the Nimrods at Kinloss and on to those at St Mawgan. Nimrod sorties are amplified by occasional contributions from Royal Naval Sea King helicopters.

In one of the earliest Tapestry sorties in January 1977, a Nimrod of 120 Squadron searched 72,000 square miles, identified and classified 165 fishing boats by nationality, position, course and speed and photographed another 95 foreign vessels. On 17 May 1978 a Nimrod of 42 Squadron from St Mawgan spotted a Spanish trawler fishing illegally, notified HM Fishery Protection Vessel *Lindisfarne* and the Spanish skipper was subsequently fined £15,000 largely on the basis of the Nimrod crew's evidence. This was the first of several such 'airborne arrests' which in 1979 led to 24 convictions being obtained by the Ministry of Agriculture, Fisheries and Food for a variety of offences by fishing vessels within the United Kingdom's fishery zone.

The Nimrod Squadrons

Nimrod crews are trained at No 236 Maritime Operational Training Unit at Royal Air Force St Mawgan in Cornwall from where they may be posted to No 42 Squadron on the same station, or to the other end of the country to Nos 120, 201 or 206 at Kinloss. Unlike other squadrons in 18 Group, No 42 has not always been in the maritime business. In World War 1 it was a Tactical Reconnaissance Squadron with the RFC in France and

Below: Offshore Tapestry — a Nimrod from the Kinloss Wing provides a reassuring presence for the crew of an oil platform in the North Sea.

Italy. In World War 2 it attacked surface shipping and laid mines in the North Sea, the Mediterranean and Indian Oceans before resuming its overland traditions in Burma. In 1952, it reformed as a maritime reconnaissance squadron flying Shackletons and served on the Beira Patrol during the blockade of Rhodesia before converting to Nimrods in 1971.

Three-quarters of the Nimrod force is, however, based at Kinloss within easy reach of the critical waters of the Eastern Atlantic and the Iceland-Faroes Gap. No 120 Squadron was formed near the end of World War 1 only but between 1941 and 1945, flying Liberators from Ireland and Iceland, sank 19 U-boats and damaged many others. After 20 years flying Shackletons it also re-equipped with Nimrod MR1s in 1971. No 201 Squadron, on the other hand, was originally No 1 Squadron of the Royal Naval Air Service which, like the other RNAS squadrons was absorbed into the Royal Air Force in April 1918 with the addition of 200 to its original squadron number. Since then, with only occasional breaks in service, it has specialised in maritime activities. It flew anti-surface and anti-submarine patrols in World War 2 and swept the Channel prior to the Normandy landings. In 1948, it contributed to the Berlin Airlift, flying its Sunderlands on to Lake Havel and with 230 Squadron was the last RAF squadron to fly the four-engined flying boat at Pembroke Dock until February 1957. After 13 years with Shackletons it became the first RAF Nimrod squadron in October 1970. The third Nimrod Squadron at Kinloss, No 206, also has RNAS roots being renumbered from RNAS No 6 in April 1918 while still a heavy bomber squadron operating in France. Since 1936, it has flown almost entirely in maritime roles. Equipped with Ansons, Hudsons, Fortresses and Liberators during World War 2 it operated off the German, Norwegian and Danish coasts as well as out over the Atlantic. During a short spell with Transport Command after the war, it also flew on the Berlin Airlift before reassuming its maritime role with Shackletons at St Eval in 1952. It re-equipped with the Nimrod at Kinloss one month after No 201 in November 1970.

Search and Rescue

In addition to its many other responsibilities, the Nimrod Force maintains one aircraft permanently at one hour's readiness for Search and Rescue (SAR) duties within the United Kingdom SAR Region which extends 1,000 miles out into the Atlantic. The Nimrod's speed, range and sensor equipment make it ideally suited to the initial crucial tasks of locating the incident and co-ordinating rescue ships and helicopters. In September 1978, for example, the crew of a ditched RNAF Atlantique were rescued by Sea King helicopters within one hour of being located by the SAR Nimrod scrambled from Kinloss. Ironically, nine members of the crew of a second Dutch Atlantique were rescued from the sea in similar manner in February 1981 when this time a Nimrod from No 42 Squadron co-ordinated the helicopter rescue.

But, naturally enough, the bulk of the actual rescues are made by the helicopters of Nos 202 and 22 Squadrons, dispersed at eight stations round the United Kingdom. Established primarily to rescue downed aircrew both RAF and RN helicopters spend far more of their time helping yachtsmen, swimmers, climbers and other civilians in distress. Successes can be spectacular but occasionally tragedy strikes, as when a winchman from No 202 Squadron Detachment at Coltishall was killed in 1980 while trying to rescue the pilot of a USAF A-10 in the North Sea.

Below: Apart from the need to keep pace with the launch and maintain a hover and not lose the casualty and overcome problems presented by gusting winds, it's all quite simple really! Aircrew learn to appreciate the value of the presence of a Sea King from No 202 Squadron.

Right: A No 202 Squadron Sea King on an overland familiarisation flight in Scotland.

Below right: Sea King of No 202 Squadron on the landing pad of RAF Coltishall, March 1980.

No 202 began to re-equip with the twin-jet Westland Sea King HAS Mk 3 in 1978, fitted with advanced all-weather search and navigation equipment enhanced by auto-pilot and on-board computer. In theory it can carry fifteen survivors in addition to its four crew members over a radius of action of about 270 miles. This alone would have marked a major increase in capacity over the previous well-tried Wessex and Whirlwinds, but on 2 October 1980 another 202 Squadron Sea King, this time from Lossiemouth, demonstrated what the aircraft could do in the hands of a determined, skilful and brave crew. In an operation lasting more than three and a half hours and despite 70ft high seas, gale force winds, flames and toxic fumes, Flight Lieutenant Michael Lakey and his crew rescued 22 survivors from the burning Swedish chemical cargo ship *Finneagle* 50 miles off the Orkneys. Not surprisingly the crew received one George Medal, one AFC, one Air Force Medal, one Queen's Commendation for valuable service in the air and one Queen's Commendation for brave conduct as well as many other awards from different sources. This rescue was, however, only a dramatic example of the long traditions of both helicopter squadrons.

No 202, originally RNAS No 2, flew fixed wing aircraft in a variety of maritime roles until 1964 when it took over the number of No 228 SAR Whirlwind Squadron at Leconfield which itself had inherited No 275's Sycamores in 1959. It is now deployed at

A Sea King of No 202 Squadron (above left) moves in to begin a 'wet winching' exercise with 'Spitfire' class *Stirling*, an RAF Rescue and Target Towing launch. Survivors may be rescued (left) by *Stirling* herself, or (above) may be picked up from a dinghy by the crewman from the Sea King and winched (right) to safety and speedy transit to the nearest medical attention.

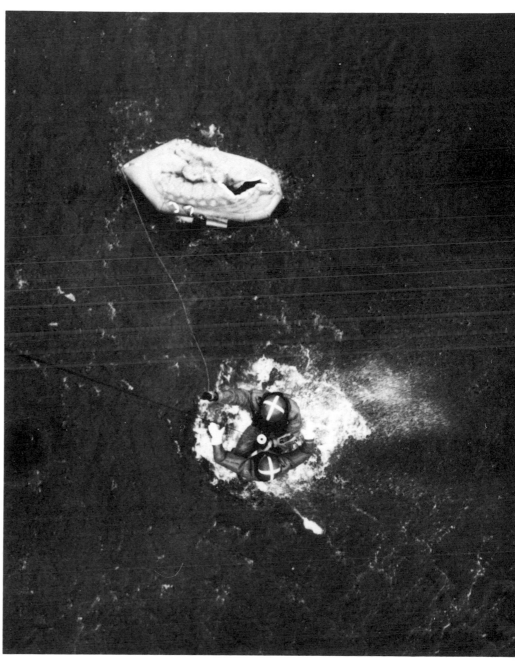

55

A mountain rescue. Above left: A climber is overdue in West Wales and an RAF Mountain Rescue Team sets out to help in the search. Above: The injured climber is located and brought to safety by the team. Left: The SAR Wessex from RAF Valley has been summoned and, despite the inhospitable terrain, the winchman is on his way down from the hovering helicopter. Right: The injured climber is winched aboard the Wessex. In a short time he will be in a hospital bed — a very fortunate man and another 18 Group statistic.

Lossiemouth, Boulmer, Leconfield and Coltishall. No 22 also originated in World War 1 and discharged fighter, reconnaissance and training duties before becoming a specialist maritime squadron in 1934. Since 1955, No 22 has flown SAR helicopters and in 1980 was deployed in flights of Whirlwinds and Wessex at Leuchars, Chivenor, Valley and Brawdy. In 1980, RAF helicopters rescued 755 people in 950 separate incidents. By 1980 studies were already being made on a possible Sea King replacement for the 1990s but in the intervening period the Sea King Force of 18 Group would continue to come to the rescue of hundreds of civilians and Servicemen all round the United Kingdom.

For both helicopters and Nimrods, every day would bring operational challenges almost identical to those expected in war except that no hostile fire would be encountered. Maritime airpower, whether locating submarines, shadowing surface vessels, identifying errant fishermen or snatching both civilian and Servicemen from disaster, would continue to protect the ocean flanks of the United Kingdom.

Below: Two new high speed launches for the Royal Air Force Marine Branch, HMAFVs *Lancaster* and *Wellington*, which will serve with other rescue/target towing launches at RAF Mount Batten. A typical job (bottom) is the recovery of a Mark 44 practice torpedo.

5

Training the People

The crest of Royal Air Force Support Command bears the inscription 'That Eagles May Fly'. By the time a pilot climbs into the cockpit of a Tornado for the first time he will have several hundred flying hours behind him, some perhaps accumulated on other fast jet operational aircraft, but always they will have begun in the flying training organisation administered from Royal Air Force Brampton: the rearing of the young eagle to the highest standards demanded by the operational commands.

Pre-Service Flying

Even before the pilot joins the Service he may have had the opportunity to fly in a Royal Air Force aircraft. As a teenager he may have sat in the back seat of a de Havilland Chipmunk T-10 of one of the 13 Air Experience Flights established throughout the United Kingdom to introduce cadets of the Air Training Corps and Combined Cadet Forces to the experience of flying. He will, however, have had the chance to do little more than gain a sense of the exhilaration of flight in a small monoplane, whereas if he were lucky enough to be accepted as a member of the University Air Squadron, he would quickly discover the real challenges facing a would-be pilot.

The University Air Squadrons

In 1925 Lord Trenchard instituted the first University Air Squadron at Cambridge. By 1981 there were 16 squadrons in the United Kingdom associated with 36 universities, 29 colleges and 11 polytechnics. They provide a military focus and unit for all RAF university cadet officers and flying training for those entering the General Duties Branch. In addition, the squadrons include Volunteer Reserve members who will also be trained to fly but who do not necessarily have a commitment to join the Service. Squadrons are staffed by regular RAF officers, all Qualified Flying Instructors (QFIs) and the squadron training programme includes groundschool training at squadron headquarters, flying training at a nearby civilian or military airfield and summer camps at operational RAF stations.

The undergraduate pilot will be expected to fit his flying into his academic curriculum without detriment to either. Each month he will be called upon to fly an 'essential exercise' check to demonstrate that he can safely complete those exercises which he has covered to a date. After he has gone solo he will be accompanied by his OFI only to check his competence. For example, a Royal Air Force VR undergraduate with 18 months' experience on the Queen's University Air Squadron at Belfast with 40 hours dual and 10 hours solo on the Bulldog could expect to do an 'essential exercise' check which would include spinning, aerobatics, stalling and a practice force-landing pattern in the local flying area of the Newtownards Peninsula south of Belfast Lough.

The detail of the sortie would begin in the squadron operations room with the met briefing by the chief instructor and the flight briefing by the student's own QFI. Then, out on to the tarmac, probably chilled by the perennial fresh breeze from the adjacent Belfast Lough, to the pre-flight check on the Bulldog. The Scottish Aviation T Mk 1 Bulldog entered service with the Central Flying School in July 1973 and is now flown by the university air squadrons and the Royal Naval Elementary Flying Training Squadrons at Leeming. It is small enough for the undergraduate to inspect thoroughly without stretching too far: 33ft wingspan, 23ft long and almost 9ft high. It is powered by a single 200hp Avco-Lycoming 10-360-A1B6 engine which gives a maximum range of 400 miles at a cruising speed of 120kts. It is a conventional side-by-side basic trainer, stable and tolerant in the air and with a comfortable landing speed of 65mph.

Below: CUAS — Cambridge University Air Squadron. Instructors and undergraduates in tight Bulldog formation over East Anglia.

Above: The Bulldog of the Squadron Commander of East Lowlands UAS flies towards Newquay from the summer camp at St Mawgan.

Centre right: Who trains the instructors who train the aircrew in the groundschools of flying units? Answer — the Ground Instructional Technique Staff at the RAF School of Education which in early 1982 completed its 500th 'GIT' course. Here potential instructors learn how to teach the intricacies of a jet engine lubrication system.

Bottom right: CFS sets the standards! Four Gazelles from the Rotary Wing at Shawbury flown by Central Flying School instructors.

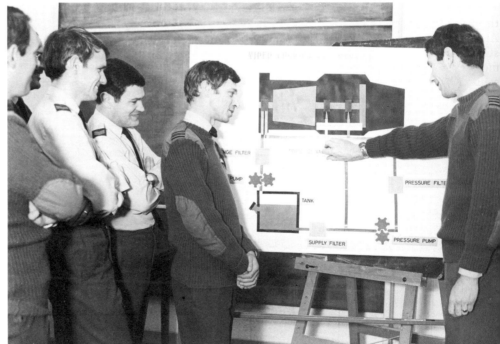

After completing the external, pre-start and pre-take-off checks this student is ready for clearance to join the airspace near Belfast. At 60kts the Bulldog is airborne and climbs at 80kts to 2,000ft to stay below Aldergrove Control Area. On this flight, as on all UAS flights the student pilot must keep a sharp lookout, not only for scheduled passenger aircraft leaving or descending towards the local airport but also for light civilian aircraft buzzing, sometimes a little unconcernedly, from nearby airfields such as Newtownards. Fortunately, however, all UAS have access to low-flying areas where such hazards are not so common. The pilot from Queens would turn south towards Donaghadee and begin to climb to about 7,000ft to begin his first exercise: the controlled spin.

The student, throughout the flying training organisation affectionately referred to as 'Bloggs', would complete his 'HASELL' checks (height, airframe, security, engine, location and lookout), rolling out of his 'lookout' turn two miles south of Donaghadee. Then the familiar sequence: maintain height, keep aircraft in balance and then at 60kts apply full rudder, control column fully back; up and over and slowly — hopefully — settling into a gentle spin. After three full turns check that the throttle is closed, the direction of the spin from the turn needle, apply full opposite rudder, push the stick fully forward until the spin stops, centralise control and ease out of the dive.

Before 'Bloggs' completed the remainder of his exercise programme he would be highly likely to experience a sudden silence, induced by his QFI to simulate engine failure. That would demand a no-warning practice force-landing pattern, and over the small fields, rolling hills and stone-walled country lanes of Northern Ireland, suitable landing areas are not easy to spot. Nevertheless, the field would be chosen, and a pattern flown which would lead to an overshoot at 150ft rather than the actual touch-down. Subsequently, return to the airfield at Sydenham by the side of the Lough would be accompanied by simulated radio failure and possibly even a further engine 'seizure'.

The exercise at Belfast resembles those flown every month at all the university air squadrons as students work towards qualification for the Preliminary Flying Badge, usually after about 35 hours. Although only a small percentage of the VR students will actually join the RAF, all will have learned a great deal about flying, about the RAF and about its contribution to the national defence. Those who do join the Service will not be taken by surprise by the exceptionally high standard set and demanded by the formal flying training schools (FTS).

The Flying Training Schools

The standards of flying training demanded at both university air squadrons and flying training schools are set at one of the oldest and most prestigious units in military aviation history. The Central Flying School (CFS), with its headquarters at Royal Air Force Leeming was formed at Upavon in 1912 and since then has trained the QFIs not only of the RAF, Royal Navy and Army but of 54 Commonwealth and Foreign Air Forces. The function of CFS is quite specific, 'To train flying instructors, on both fixed and rotary wing aircraft who, by their skill, knowledge and enthusiasm, will help to maintain the flying efficiency of the RAF at the highest level'. Fixed wing students complete some 85 hours flying instruction in 25 weeks while potential helicopter instructors complete 70 hours in 13 weeks. Fast jet training on the Hawk is carried out at RAF Valley and helicopter flying takes place at RAF Shawbury on the Gazelle.

Nor does an instructor's development finish when he graduates from CFS. He will be awarded a B-2 or exceptionally a B-1 instructor category but at least once a year thereafter he will be examined and recategorised by members of the Examining Wing of CFS. The Wing, a component of CFS since 1927, ensures that instructional methods throughout the flying training organisation remain at the highest standard and that new ideas and techniques are co-ordinated and disseminated.

CFS also administers and supervises what the Royal Air Force unequivocally assumes to be the most accomplished aerobatic team in the world: the nine members of the Red Arrows. In 1980 they gave 119 displays in four countries. They epitomise the discipline, skill, teamwork and sheer professionalism which has been the pride of the Royal Air Force since its earliest days and which permeates all squadrons whether regularly in the public eye or not.

After graduating from CFS the majority of instructors will be posted to one of the FTS or UAS administered by RAF Support Command. In 1981, all initial officer training was carried out at the RAF College. Thereafter, direct entrant would-be pilots without the requisite previous flying experience underwent 15 hours flying on the Chipmunk at the Flying Selection Squadron to select those with suitable aptitude to start basic flying training.

Direct entrants with the requisite previous flying experience and those who pass the flying selection, start the basic flying training course on the Jet Provost 3A at either Linton-on-Ouse or Church Fenton, or on the Jet Provost 5A at Cranwell. The basic phase of the direct entry basic flying training course comprises 97 hours flying and lasts 37 weeks.

The British Aerospace Jet Provost T3A entered service with the RAF in 1959. Powered by a Rolls-Royce Viper Mk 102 turbojet producing 1,750lb static thrust, it is unpressurised, has a maximum level flight speed of 326mph and a range of 565 miles. The more powerful T5A has a pressurised cockpit, modified airframe, maximum level flight speed of 440mph and a range of 900 miles.

Entrants from the university air squadrons will normally have completed 95 hours on the Bulldog and will stay at Cranwell to fly a further 77 on the JP-5A on the graduate entrant basic flying training course. Their basic phase last 31 weeks.

On completion of the basic phase, all pilots are streamed according to their aptitudes, the needs of the Service and, where possible, personal inclinations, to fast jet, multi-engine or helicopter aircraft. In view of the front-line configuration of the RAF, the great majority of pilots will embark on the route which will ultimately lead to Harrier, Jaguar, Phantom, Buccaneer or Tornado. They will first complete 61 hours on the JP-5A at Cranwell, then move to No 4 FTS at Valley to begin 85 advanced flying hours on the British Aerospace (Hawker Siddeley) Hawk T1. Powered by a single Rolls Royce/Turbomeca RT172.06.11

Adour 851 turbofan engine, Hawk has a maximum level flight speed of 540kts and a range of 690 miles. Stressed to +8 and −4g, Hawk was designed to be fully aerobatic but it is also simpler to understand and easier to fly in the elementary stages than its predecessor, the Folland Gnat. Consequently, it has quickly achieved considerable popularity with students and instructors alike and conversion times have been cut, thereby leaving more syllabus hours for applied exercises such as low-flying navigation or formation. Training can therefore be more heavily weighted towards the skills essential to a later operational environment. Its increased range permits a student to fly more complex series of exercises which allow him to experience a longer and heavier cockpit workload than was possible on the Gnat. Moreover, the aircraft was designed from the outset as an advanced trainer; it is of rugged construction and has a long fatigue life which should ensure that it continues into service well into the 1990s. In that period it can be readily modified to carry more advanced avionic equipment such as a simple head-up display or offset TACAN by which to simulate INAS operation. Thereby, the gap between advanced flying training and conversion to the next generation of fast jet operational aircraft will be reduced still further. After successful completion of the Valley course, pilots would move on to one of the tactical weapon units at Chivenor or Brawdy to prepare for their ultimate emergence as tyro combat pilots at the operational conversion units.

If, on the other hand, the student pilot had been selected for the Nimrod, Hercules, Vulcan or Victor fleets, his development

attern would differ appropriately. After completing his basic
hase he would spend another 27 hours lead-in training on the
P3A or 5A before going to Finningley, the RAF's centre for
multi-engine and multi-crew training. There, he would remain for
0 weeks, during which he would spend 6 weeks in groundschool
earning about the Jetstream, meteorology, flight planning and
ircrew survival. He would spend 45 hours in the air and up to
nother 45 in the flight simulator. He would also begin to learn
hat he was not only to be responsible for an airframe and a
mission. He would not have the high speed low-level demands of
is colleagues at Valley but he would become aware of the
esponsibilities of captaincy: leadership within an aircraft, as
pposed to leadership of other crews in other aircraft.

The British Aerospace (Scottish Aviation) Jetstream T Mk 1
as been in service with the RAF from November 1976. It is used
y the Multi Engine Training Squadron at RAF Finningley, both
o train student pilots in the multi-engined role and to provide
efresher training for RAF pilots who are returning to operational
les.

The RAF Jetstream is powered by two Turbomeca Astazou 16
urboprops which each provide 985 EHP for take-off. The fully
ressurised aircraft provides flight deck seating for instructor and
udent pilots with a third seat for an additional crew member.
he fuselage provides for up to four additional passengers. The
ght deck is equipped with a comprehensive range of VHF and
HF communications, navigation instrumentation and modern
ght instrumentation which includes the Sperry Stars Flight

Director System. It has a cruising speed of 215kts and a range of
up to 1,200nm.

Helicopter Training

The third group of pilots to be streamed in the later stages of their
flying training will go to the helicopter force. Unlike their
colleagues staying in the fixed wing environment, they will leave
the JP3A or 5A on completion of their basic phase and move to
No 2 FTS at Shawbury. There, they will spend 28 weeks flying
the Gazelle and Wessex helicopters before, like their fixed wing
contemporaries, they are awarded their wings on successful
completion of their advanced flying stage. They fly 76 hours on
the Anglo-French Gazelle HT MR 3, which although light and
small has a cruising speed of 140mph and a range of some 400
miles, followed by a further 50 hours on the heavier Westland
Wessex Mk 60. The search and rescue element of the training will
be carried out at Valley, where Snowdonia and the Irish Sea
provide training areas which frequently call for full operational
sorties. Although the new pilots will all graduate to one of the
helicopter OCUs, they will not necessarily spend the whole of
their flying careers on rotary wing aircraft, anymore than their

fixed wing colleagues will remain on one type. And, unless they fly only Harriers or Jaguars, they will sooner or later learn to fly as a team with navigators, who have their own training pattern after completion of initial officer training.

Navigator Training

The role of the navigator in the Royal Air Force changed a great deal between 1960 and 1980 and the demands upon him in the next decade are unlikely to decrease. In all aircraft his equipment has become more sophisticated which on the one hand has reduced some of the time traditionally allocated to the 'mechanical' aspect of calculation and plotting, but at the same time has called for swifter reactions and greater co-ordination and analysis of information. But of greater significance have been the challenges posed by high speed low level flight: regularly in the Buccaneer, Phantom, Vulcan and Canberra and frequently in the Nimrod. In the 1980s, the challenge will be heightened dramatically as the Tornado GR1 assumes its multi-role operations, while the F2 will maintain the demand for the interceptor navigators and the transport and helicopter forces will continue to require operational skills worldwide.

Consequently, as navigation training at Finningley entered the 1980s it was being modified to prepare most effectively for what would be a considerable variety of tasks. Whereas previously aspiring navigators spent 16 weeks on Bulldogs and 'academics', 26 weeks (77 hours) on the British Aerospace Dominie T1 and six weeks (15 hours) on the JP3A before streaming for advanced low or high level training, now the basic phase has been reduced to 29 weeks (44 hours Dominie and 20 hours Jet Provost) followed by a more role-orientated advanced phase of 22 weeks which will allow for stream switching if required when a student's provisional posting is known. In all phases of the course, extensive use is made of the Dominie ground simulator.

Airborne exercises may start at 35,000ft at a little over 200kts. While radar is the navigator's primary positional aid, he must

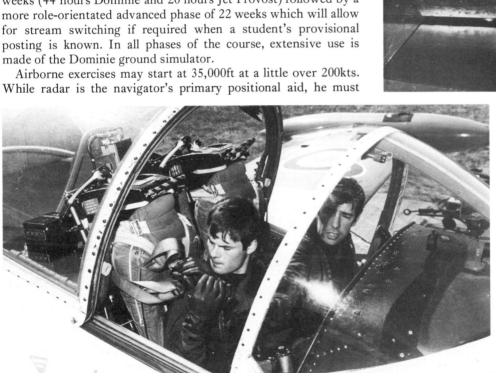

Above: Navigator training at Finningley. An instructor in the Ground School explains the details of an Echo 190 cloud-collision warning radar.

Centre left: Learning the trade of fast jet navigator at Finningley. A student dons his harness in a Jet Provost 5B before beginning a low level navigation exercise.

Bottom left: Final preparations for a navigational training flight at Finningley. Groundcrew check the Dominie prior to groundstart while the navigators compare final notes.

Right: A syndicate of the RAF Staff College, Bracknell grapples with the problems of air power in the modern world. Here, an exchange officer from the British Army on the directing staff draws out the opinions of Indian, US and RAF students.

learn all the traditional techniques and gradually learn to deal with the pressures and procedures of crowded airways and unscheduled diversions. Later he will fly at 1,000ft in the Jet Provost, learning mental dead reckoning techniques using only topographical maps and a stopwatch. Gradually, he will fly lower, until at 250ft his tasks will be increased to include radio calls, look-out and fuel management in addition to his navigation. In the advanced phases, role specialisation will determine whether the student increases his low level reactions and responsibilities or concentrates on the complexities of astro-navigation, limited aids and airways restrictions. In a very few months one might find himself at night at 600ft 500 miles out over the Atlantic, another slipping into a narrow Himalayan valley, another negotiating crowded airways of the Eastern Seaboard of the United States and another following the contours of a Scottish snowscape at 400kts: and all can expect the same question — 'Where are we, nav?' In Tornado he will be given much more technical assistance, but much less time in which to apply it.

Meanwhile, all three variants of Nimrod, the Hercules, the Victors, Vulcans and VC-10s will continue to need additional crew members: the air engineers, air electronics operators and other specialists. These also will continue to be trained at Finningley before moving on to the precise crew skill training at the operational conversion units, such as those at St Mawgan or Lyneham.

Ground Training

It is a truism that any aircrew can only be as good as their equipment and supporting groundcrew permit them to be. Since the days when Lord Trenchard stressed the importance of giving airmen the best possible training — even to the extent of allocating the sumptuous Halton House to his new apprentices rather than to senior officers for a staff college that precept has guided first Training Command and now the training units in RAF Support Command.

Even before joining the RAF, some 35,000 young men in about 1,000 Air Training Corps Units throughout the United Kingdom are given air experience flying and gliding in the 13 air experience flights and 27 gliding schools, under the control of the Air Officer Commanding Air Cadets. Each year about 20,000 Servicemen and women pass through 500 different ground training courses preparing or advancing them for 150 trades in 19 main trade groups, or if commissioned, for specialist engineering, supply, air traffic control, secretarial, police and educational duties.

Staff Training

A junior RAF officer will usually be fully occupied with developing his or her specialist competence and executive ability. With increasing seniority, however, will come the assumption of wider responsibilities which will in turn demand a greater breadth and depth of knowledge about his own Service, the Royal Navy, Army and ultimately our Allies. The first step for a flight lieutenant will be the Officers' Command School at RAF Henlow where he will learn about the broader challenges of junior command. Later he will expand his staff skills by completing an individual staff studies course. As a squadron leader he may be selected for the six weeks basic staff course and, ultimately, as a senior squadron leader or wing commander, he may be one of the 50 or so officers who are selected each year to attend the Advanced Staff Course at Bracknell, which will prepare him for the highest positions in the Royal Air Force.

Indeed, it is only the training organisation as a whole of the Royal Air Force that can guarantee the future quality of the Service. If the aircrew are highly skilled, if the groundcrews are equally dedicated and competent and if the command and staff skills of the senior officers are good enough to draw out the greatest effectiveness from both, then the RAF can confidently recall the Greek saying: 'It's the men who make the city, not the walls'.

Initial Officer Training

The first step on the road towards a commission in the Royal Air Force is Initial Officer Training at the Royal Air Force College, Cranwell. Left: It can be a hard road for officer cadets of either sex as they face practical problems in field exercises before (above) reaching the moment of graduation.

Right: Preparing to go solo — a student pilot receives final words of encouragement from his instructor at Cranwell as he straps into a BAe Jet Provost T5.

Flying Training School

Left: 'You have it Bloggs'. A Jet Provost from 7FTS, Church Fenton begins a starboard break.

Below: Multi-engine training. A Scottish Aviation Jetstream T1 from 6FTS begins a wintry let down back to Finningley.

Right: A pairs take-off by two Provost T3As from 1FTS, Linton-on-Ouse.

Below right: Groundcrew assist a student to strap into a Hawk at 4TFS, Valley.

Below, far right: Ejection seat repairs on a Hawk at Valley.

Tactical Weapons Unit

By the time a pilot leaves RAF Valley he has learned to fly fast jets. At one of the Tactical Weapons Units he begins to learn to attack. Above left: Meeting some of the equipment; (above) tactics; (left) briefing for a ground attack sortie; (above right) it might be the same sort of aircraft he flew at Valley, but now it's a weapons system — here with rocket pod dispensers; (right) rigorous debriefing forms part of the continual pursuit for operational excellence.

Below: Hawk T1s from the TWU, RAF Brawdy.

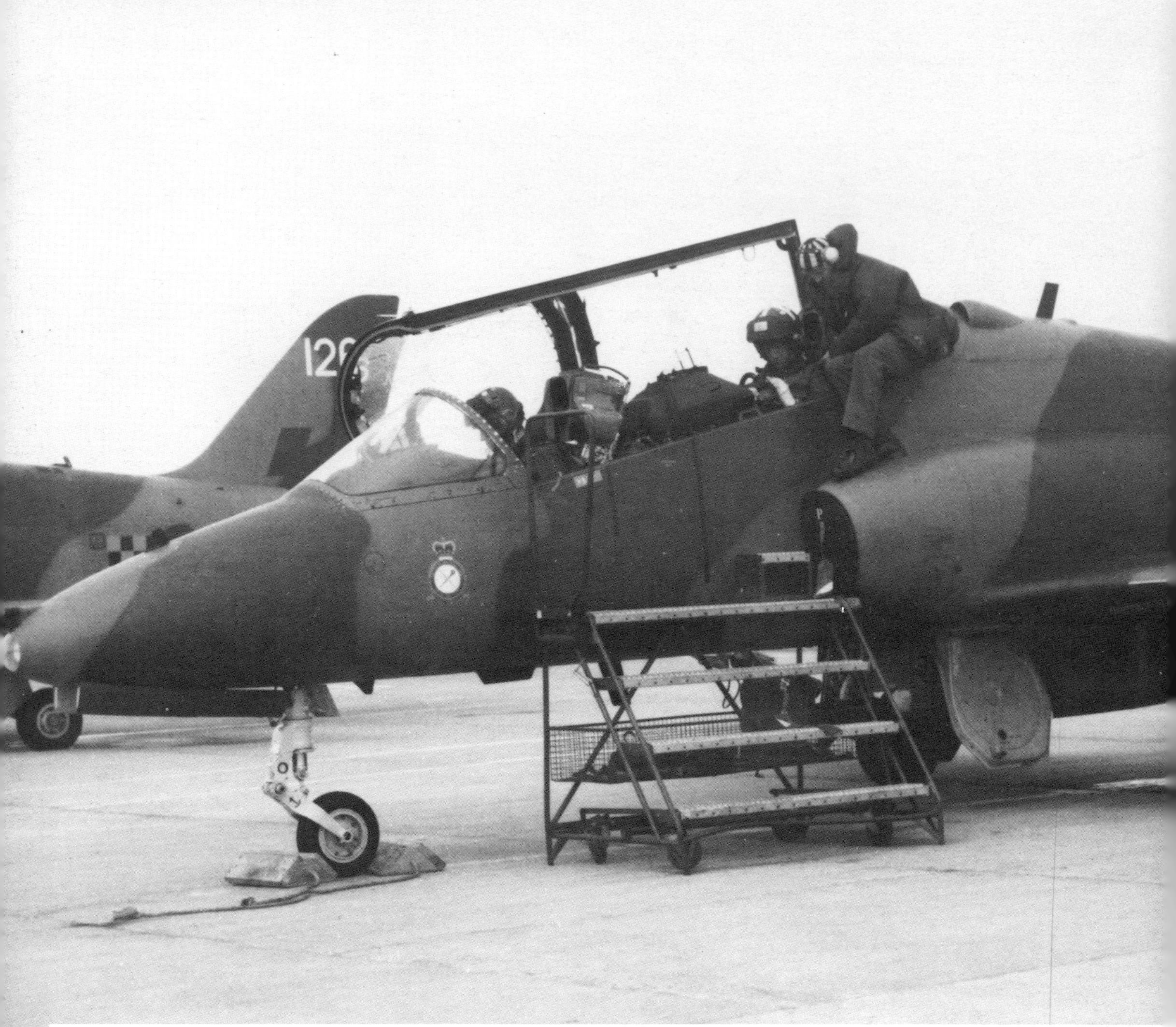

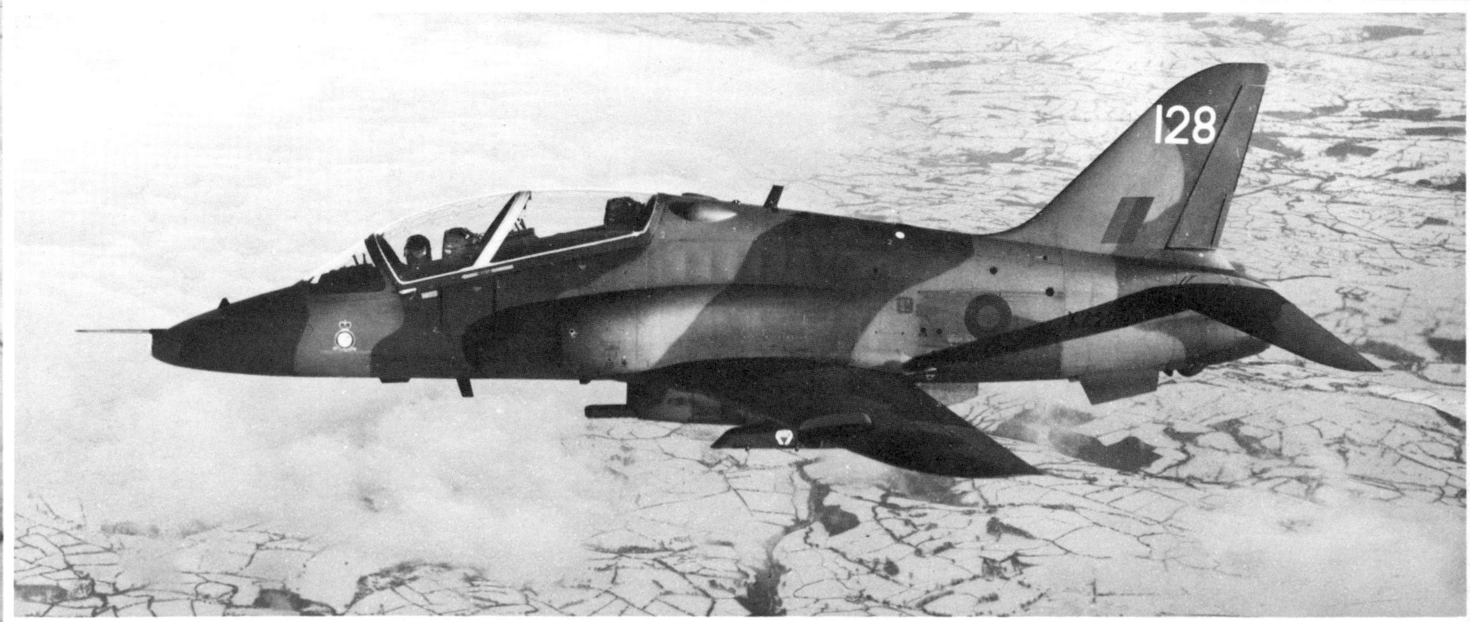

A 4FTS Hawk T1 from RAF Valley banking steeply over a Welsh valley.
CO1

Jaguars of No 6 Squadron over the Isle of Wight. *COI*

A Nimrod MR2, XV228, seen during a sortie from RAF Kinloss. *BAe*

Tornado ZA552 of the Tornado Weapons Conversion Unit in a hardened aircraft shelter at RAF Honington, Suffolk. The station has 12 HASs that enable aircraft to be serviced, armed and refuelled under protective cover. *Allan Burney*

Two views of Harrier XV738, the first production standard single-seater subsequently modified to GR3 standard and equipped with laser rangefinder nose, and seen here in service with No 3 Squadron. In the upper photo four SNEB rocket pods are salvoed at a range target in Sardinia; below, a short take-off from a road during an exercise in Germany. *BAe*

Finding out how it works, and how to repair it.
Left: An Apprentice at RAF Cosford learns
about aircraft controls on a 'retired' Argosy
previously flown by No 115 Squadron; (below)
No 1 School of Technical Training, Halton.

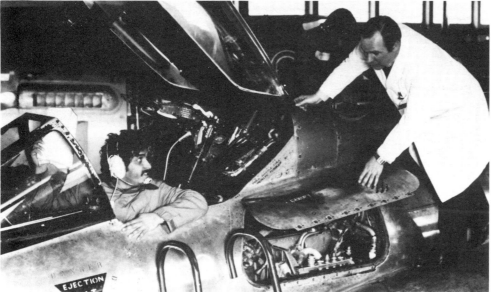

Above: Training on engine maintenance of the Tornado's Turbo-Union RB199 at the TTTE, RAF Cottesmore.

Centre left: Cooperation with foreign air forces — Saudi Arabian groundcrew learn about the Lightning at Cosford.

Bottom left: Used for both RAF training and international competition — the indoor arena at Cosford.

Top right: Flight test for a veteran — the traditional swing of the propeller for a Chipmunk of the Air Experience Flight prior to take-off from RAF Abingdon.

Right: The Harrier isn't *that* easy to fly! A product of the RAF Police Dog Training School at Newton with its handler, having a close check on security of a No 4 Squadron Harrier in a wood somewhere in northern Germany.

Far right: From training in the Catering School at Hereford to the support of the inner man on the operational station.

The Red Arrows

The precision and harmony of the Red Arrows, as they are known the world over, belies the fact that in war the colourful red paint would be replaced by camouflage and the smoke dispensers by air-to-ground weapons.

6

Royal Air Force Germany

Most of the aircrew and groundcrew emerging from the training units, with the exception of the transport and maritime specialists, are likely to serve sooner or later on one of the stations in Royal Air Force Germany, known familiarly throughout the Service as 'RAFG'. The Royal Air Force presence in Germany dates back to World War 2 when, as the Second Tactical Air Force it supported the Allied Armies in the later months of the war on the Continent. Remaining as part of the British Forces of Occupation, it assumed its present title in 1959.

Throughout the RAF there is no lack of understanding of the fact that peacetime preparedness is an indispensable element to deterrence to war, but on RAFG units one becomes conscious very quickly of the proximity of the potential enemy. The Command Headquarters in the forests at Rheindahlen is only 30 minutes 'Flogger' flying time from the Inner German Border (IGB). Gutersloh, on the eastern side of the Rhine, is only half that distance. Consequently, the German bases have been given first priority in the provision of hardened shelters (HAS) for all combat aircraft, and in the 'toning down' programme which has resulted in all buildings, runways and taxiways being painted or coated to give a dull green finish. Stations are encircled with barbed wire and sand-bagged emplacements, to leave no visitor in doubt, as the notice by Bruggen gate has it: 'The task of this station in peace is to train for war'. The forthright character of the commanding officer who installed this notice is commemorated by the next few words ' . . . and don't you forget '. Such a notice would be appropriate for any base in RAFG.

The Front Line
RAFG is at once the forward defence of the United Kingdom and is the front line of NATO forces in Central Europe. Unlike the Commands at home which are divided and organised according to their function, RAFG is almost a complete air force in miniature embracing air defence, attack, strike, reconnaissance and communication squadrons, together with its own maintenance unit and hospital. The units are located on four main bases: Wildenrath, Bruggen, Laarbruch and Gutersloh in addition to the Headquarters at Rheindahlen and the hospital at Wegberg.

Air Defence
Wildenrath, on the west bank of the Rhine near Rheindahlen is the home of Nos 19 and 92 Fighter Squadrons, equipped with Phantom FGR-2s. No 19 Squadron has one of the proudest records in the RAF. It accounted for 281 enemy aircraft in World War 1 after its formation on 1 September 1915 and, after being the first squadron to receive the Spitfire in 1938, shot down a further 145 in World War 2. It has been equipped with the FGR2 Phantom at Wildenrath since January 1977. No 92 Squadron followed No 19 to Wildenrath in April 1977 and it also has a distinguished history. After service in World War 1, it was a

Below: Phantom FGR2 of No 19 Squadron based at RAF Wildenrath displays its new all-grey paint scheme.

notable participant in the Battle of Britain, flying from Biggin Hill. Among its famous pilots were Wing Commander A. G. 'Sailor' Milan and Flight Lieutenant Bob Stanford Tuck. By the end of the war the Squadron claimed $317\frac{1}{2}$ enemy aircraft destroyed. Now, both Squadrons combine in peacetime to carry out a commitment retained by the United Kingdom under the terms of the Bonn Convention to defend the integrity of the airspace over the northern half of the Federal Republic of Germany, as well as to contribute to SACEUR's comprehensive air defence provision in the Central Region of Allied Command Europe.

Consequently, like their colleagues in 11 Group in the United Kingdom, the aircrews of Nos 19 and 92 Squadrons maintain aircraft on constant states of immediate readiness to scramble to intercept unidentified aircraft trespassing in the 'Air Defence Identification Zone', an invisible barrier stretching down the Western side of the border with East Germany. 'Battle Flight' is scrambled on average twice a week, sometimes as a practice, sometimes for real. Within seconds of the klaxon's wailing, the two Spey engines with the after-burners in will give the Phantoms 18,000lb of thrust down Wildenrath's runway, yet the crews will not know whether the scramble is a practice called by sector control centre or a response to a real intrusion from across the frontier. In either case, they will be armed with four radar-guided Sparrow and four infra-red homing Sidewinder missiles and a 20mm six-barrel cannon able to fire 1,000 rounds a minute. In peacetime, they will remain under ground control until the intruder is within range of the aircraft's own all-weather radar. Thereafter, the radar navigator in the back seat will vector the fighter into a position from which the pilot can make a visual identification. Under other conditions, of course, and subject to the rules of engagement in force at the time, the Phantom would be positioned to attack with the appropriate weapon system. So far, the culprits have not come from across the border: they are sometimes private aircraft off track or occasionally civilian airliners with a faulty identification transponder. But, whatever their height, speed and type, they are very vulnerable. The combination of long range, look-down, all-weather radar, two-man crew and weapon mix make the FGR-2s of Nos 19 and 92

Squadrons formidable opponents at either high or low level. This constant national requirement for the Battle Flight ensures a very high peacetime readiness state which enhances the Squadrons preparation for their wartime role under SACEUR. A large proportion of squadron training is allocated to low level interception, working not only with other Phantoms, but with Harriers, Buccaneers, Jaguars and Allied aircraft. Together with F-15s, F-16s, F-104s and Allied F-4s the Wildenrath Phantom make a major contribution to the Alliance's deterrent posture.

In the near future, the Sparrow will be replaced by Sky Flash and the current Sidewinder by the even more agile AIM-9L. Later, the FGR2s may be supplemented by Tornado F2s and by aircraft procured to the Air Staff Target 410 (AST-410) which will have an air superiority responsibility as well as an offensive support role. Among the options for AST-410 are the McDonnell Douglas F-18 Hornet, a European collaborative project tentatively referred to as the European Combat Aircraft or 'ECA' and a wholly British design.

The Surface-to-Air Defences

NATO's air defences are, of course, not dependent on the manned interceptor. The belt of Allied surface-to-air missiles running from the Baltic to the Austrian border, known by its components as the Nike-Hawk system, is complemented by two weapons deployed by RAFG. No 25 Squadron operates the Bloodhound Mk medium and high altitude surface-to-air missile (SAM). Previously, the Squadron had a long and distinguished night/all weather fighter record. Since 1970, the Squadron has been deployed with Bloodhounds in Germany. The missiles are transportable but were located in 1970 at Bruggen, Laarbruch and Wildenrath to capitalise in peacetime on existing logistic and administrative support. The weapon's radius of action, of course extends considerably beyond the immediate airspace round the airfields. Its semi-active homing guidance system makes particularly invulnerable to electronic countermeasures, indeed such activity could well actually enhance the weapon's accuracy.

Short-range, low-level SAM defence is provided by the British Aerospace/Marconi Rapier. During the last decade, the offensive aircraft of Frontal Aviation, the tactical arm of the Soviet A

Forces, have greatly increased their range and payload. Sukhoi Su-17 'Fitter-D' Mikoyan MiG23 'Flogger-G' and Mikoyan MiG27 'Flogger-J' now present a qualitative and quantitative low-level threat which was simply not present 10 years previously. In view of the essential contribution which airpower must make to NATO strategy, it is to be expected that airfields will be high priority targets for Warsaw Pact aircraft. If they should penetrate the fighter screen, the Nike-Hawk belt and the Bloodhound area they will be met by four Rapier Squadrons of No 4 Wing of the RAF Regiment, one of which is based at Wildenrath and the others at Laarbruch, Bruggen and Gutersloh. Each Rapier Squadron has eight fire units with four missiles on line at each unit. The units are fully mobile and quickly dispersed to locations away from the airfields in times of tension, which would permit low-level intercept of high speed attacking aircraft before they reached their missile launch point. Each unit is equipped with Identification Friend or Foe (IFF) systems and the recent addition of the Marconi DM 1818 'Blindfire' radar has added an all-weather and night capability to the original optical system. Indeed, the cover provided by the Rapier Squadrons is now so comprehensive that, in 1982, the Bloodhound units are expected to be redeployed to the United Kingdom.

Left: Phantom FGR2 of No 92 Squadron from RAF Wildenrath.

Right: Bloodhound surface-to-air missile of No 25 Squadron, RAF Wildenrath.

Below: Replacement Bloodhound SAMs in RAF Germany.

So, although Wildenrath has a primary responsibility for air defence the SAM supporting elements are deployed to all main bases and all the RAFG air defence units are co-ordinated with the NATO system. One other unit at Wildenrath, however, has a very different responsibility. The title and honourable fighter combat tradition of No 60 Squadron were assumed by the RAFG Communication Squadron in 1969. No 60, established in 1916 and including among its aces Billy Bishop and Albert Ball, had served for almost all its time in the Far East before 'arriving' in Germany when the Ministry of Defence decided to perpetuate the most distinguished squadron numbers and associations. The Communication Squadron itself had been established to move special passengers and freight during and after the invasion of Normandy and, in fact, brought General Montgomery to France three days later. Now, the Squadron flies the twin-engined Percival Pembroke between units in Germany, United Kingdom and along the air corridors to and from West Berlin. In 1970, the wings of all Pembrokes were re-sparred and the light communications aircraft are likely to be seen in European skies for a good many years yet.

Offensive Operations

A few miles to the west of Wildenrath, on the German-Dutch border, is RAF Bruggen, the largest of the RAFG bases and the home of the Command's Jaguar fighter-bomber wing. To a cursory glance the layout is similar to the home of Nos 19 and 92 Squadrons. The airfield is likely to appear deserted except for the two or three Jaguars actually taxying, landing or preparing for take-off. All the others are out of sight in the HAS which are scattered among the pine woods around the airfield. In peacetime there is a great deal of administrative and support activity which would abruptly terminate upon the threat of war. But there the resemblance with Wildenrath ceases because Bruggen's task is not defensive but to launch the aircraft which would take the war back to the invader.

The first Jaguar GR1 deployed to Bruggen in 1975 and there are now four squadrons in the Wing: Nos 14, 17, 20 and 31 Squadrons. If the Warsaw Pact ground forces should ever cross the Inner German Border, the Bruggen Wing would be swiftly and heavily engaged. By 1980 the Warsaw Pact armies enjoyed considerable local numerical superiority in Central Europe over in-place NATO ground forces, especially in tanks, armoured personnel carriers and artillery. The task of NATO tactical offensive aircraft would be to redress that imbalance by providing air support to the defending armies, by attacking enemy formations as they deployed towards the battlefield and by dislocating and disrupting further reinforcements along their lines of march. The Jaguar's range superiority over the F-104, F-5, F-16 and Phantom make it a most valuable asset to SACEUR for use in such operations.

But, at the same time as the offensive strength of the Warsaw Pact Air Forces has risen, so a large number of surface-to-air defences have been deployed which can now move forward with their ground forces. The tracked four barrel ZSU-23 radar-laid guns, the SAM 4, 6, 8, 9, 10, 11 and 13s, some guided by radar, some by infra-red heat-seeking systems — comprise a formidable array which the Jaguars must penetrate to reach their objectives. Indeed, for the foreseeable future, the greater threat to the Allied aircraft near the battlefield is likely to come from surface fire rather than from fighters. The MiG-23 'Flogger' series, for example, has as yet only a very limited look-down capability and 'Foxbat-A' had none. Even when the Warsaw Pact aircraft do come to use pulse doppler airborne intercept radars and, therefore, improve their ability to pick up swiftly moving targets against ground clutter, the problem of producing and firing a very low level air-to-air missile will still remain.

To operate under such demanding circumstances, therefore, the Jaguar crews train to fly down to 250ft at 500kts and, if necessary, both lower and faster. Its small size makes it a difficult target and its twin Adour engines leave no tell-tale smoke plumes. It is armed with 30mm Aden guns and can deliver cluster weapons, free-fall 500lb or 1,000lb bombs, laser-guided bombs or, should their use be authorised by the political leaders of NATO, nuclear weapons. Its navigational and weapon aiming sub-system (NAVWASS) incorporates a head-up-display projected on the canopy in front of the pilot and may be pre-programmed with wind speeds at height, way points, initial point prior to making the attack run, target position and much more information which, in previous generations, would have taxed a navigator and bomb-aimer to the full. Moreover, the NAVWASS has been greatly improved since its first installation, the black boxes on which it depends are steadily being reduced in size. The laser ranger and marked target seeker may be used with a forward air controller equipped with a laser target marker. When the aircraft approaches the target it is illuminated by the laser beam of the target marker. The Marked Target Seeker in the aircraft automatically acquires and tracks the laser energy reflected from the target, driving the pilot's head-up-display to indicate target position in elevation and azimuth. The distance to the target is then measured automatically and, even if the target is not being illuminated the airborne equipment may still be used as a range-finder. Consequently, the pilot's search task is reduced and he may not actually need to see his target at all. The aircraft demands great precision from its crews, not simply because of the need for navigation and bombing accuracy, but because many missions could comprise eight or more aircraft, and timing over the target must be exact to the second to reduce the efficiency of the defences, increase the impact of the raid and, indeed, to reduce the chances of air-to-air accidents. Not surprisingly, therefore, competition between the four Jaguar Squadrons is extremely keen and standards high. No 14, located in Germany since 1946, was the first to operate the new aircraft in April 1975. No 14 has spent most of its RAF service overseas either in the Middle East or in Germany and during World War 1 had a detachment of aircraft working with the guerilla forces of Lawrence of Arabia. No 17 which also began to re-equip with Jaguars in 1975, has a long history of fighter-ground attack which includes a famous sortie in World War 1 by the then Second Lieutenant John Slessor against 200 mounted Turkish troops. No 20, which took its Jaguars in 1977 has served almost entirely overseas since its formation in 1915 and, since 1932, mainly in the offensive support role. No 31 Squadron, on the other hand, discharged a variety of tasks between its formation at Farnborough in 1915 and its conversion to Jaguars at Bruggen in 1976, including transport and photographic reconnaissance. In June 1980, it was demonstrated that previous variety was no bar to current effectiveness when Flight Lieutenant Ian Kenyon won the Broadhurst Trophy for low-level shallow angle bombing and achieved the best individual score for visual lay-down bombing in the biennial Tactical Air Meet held at the USAF's Ramstein Air Force Base, competing against other highly professional crews from Belgium, Canada, West Germany, Norway, the United States and France.

Such competition is one of the ways in which the Bruggen squadrons can demonstrate their constant high state of effectiveness which, as in the case of their interceptor colleagues is the best way of reducing the likelihood that they will be tested in war. Such a Meet is not solely or, indeed, primarily competition. It is an opportunity for NATO crews to work together on various kinds of offensive sorties in a simulated hostile environment of 'enemy' aircraft, SAMs and electronic countermeasures, while supported by 'friendly' reconnaissance and electronic counter countermeasures and other kinds of defence suppression. Jaguar is, of course, equipped with integral hostile radar warning equipment. After 12 tactical missions in the Air Meet the national units were separated and, after drawing lots, reformed with international teams for the two competitive missions designed to test weapons delivery, navigation and tactical reconnaissance. In 1980, the competition also included a

Above: Jaguar GR1 of No 20 Squadron comes in to land at RAF Bruggen, carrying underwing fuel tanks on inboard pylons and a practice bomb canister on the central fuselage pylon.

Right: Ground defence in war would be largely the responsibility of ground tradesmen and officers. Here a sector defensive position is deployed during a TACEVAL at a station in RAFG.

operational turn round to give the ground crews an opportunity to demonstrate the skills without which the best pilot in the world could achieve nothing. Dispersal of aircraft to HAS has, of course, put an additional premium on the teamwork which can refuel, rearm and service an aircraft in the shortest possible time.

However, the Bruggen crews do not have to wait for a biennial exercise to demonstrate their effectiveness. Because NATO is entirely a defensive Alliance and because in any conflict the Warsaw Pact could expect to have the advantage of choosing the time, place and method of the attack, it is highly likely that the Bruggen Wing would first be fighting over West German territory to stop the invading forces. Consequently, the Jaguars can fly regularly over the roads and fields where they will be likely to operate until every contour becomes familiar to the crews. Longer sorties can be simulated by attacks on training ranges either in Western Europe, back in the United Kingdom or on the NATO range at Decimomannu in Sardinia. In addition, they will participate in the Red and Maple Flag exercises in North America which are described in Chapter 9. And, of course, closer to home, the Jaguars demonstrate their ability to maintain operations even should Bruggen's runways be temporarily damaged by recovering to autobahns and using taxiways for both take-off and landing.

And, in common with all the other NATO squadrons deployed in AAFCE, they must face the rigours of TACEVAL: the no-notice simulation of a full wartime alert. The tactical evaluations serve four main purposes: to assess the ability of RAF units to meet their operational tasks, to ascertain if any deficiencies exist, to report to the Commander-in-Chief RAFG on the operational effectiveness of his forces and to report to SACEUR on the status of RAF units which are assigned to Allied Command Europe. TACEVAL tests not only the preparedness and operational effectiveness of the aircrew, but the strength of the logistic and other supporting facilities and the ability of all elements of the unit to survive and operate in hostile air and ground conditions.

As if the approximately annual TACEVAL was not enough, station commanders will order their own periodic evaluations which will demand standards at least as high as those set by the NATO teams. An extremely important by-product of the TACEVAL system has been to emphasise how essential it is for everyone on a station to work together as a war-fighting team. Indeed it is possible for a station to produce the best possible operational effectiveness results in TACEVAL and still receive a very critical unsatisfactory overall assessment if its supporting elements have been found wanting. Happily, RAFG stations have never had such an embarrassment. Indeed, they have consistently achieved the best evaluation standards of any units in the Central Region.

One larger unit at Bruggen is in the unenviable position of getting caught by a TACEVAL on all four major RAF units. No 431 MU is responsible for the second-line servicing of a large proportion of the air and ground equipment used throughout the Command. In the event of tension, it would deploy its people and kit around the four main airfields. While it was moving out, elements of squadrons from the Royal Engineers would be moving in to join prepositioned rapid runway repair facilities on each main operational base. The dependence of RAFG on soldiers to ensure that damaged runways are swiftly repaired is an appropriate reminder that Air Force and Army are co-located in Germany to combine their resources in both defence and offence in the most effective way to sustain deterrence and, if ever deterrence should fail, to deny an aggressor his objectives.

The Jaguar punch is being further strengthened by the acquisition of Paveway laser-guided bombs. This modern edition of the 'smart' bomb used in South East Asia has a self-contained guidance unit and power supplies enclosed in a fixture which can be added to a traditional 1,000lb bomb. The target can be illuminated from either the ground or from the air. The considerable increase in accuracy made possible by the Paveway system not only produces enormous increases in the cost-effectiveness of bombing missions, but can be used with very great precision against selected targets. Night attack capability may be further enhanced by the installation of self-contained target identification equipment such as the forward looking infra-red systems currently under development in the Royal Air Force. Later, the Jaguars themselves will be replaced either by the aircraft procured to AST-410 or by the IDS variant of Tornado after it has re-equipped the longer range squadrons based at Laarbruch.

Longer Range Offensive Operations

Since 1972, Laarbruch has been the home of Nos XV and 16 Squadrons flying Buccaneer SMK2s. Powered by two Rolls-Royce Spey Bypass turbo-jet engines developing over 11,000lb of thrust each, the Buccaneer has the 'longest legs' and carries the heaviest payload of 16,000lb of any of the aircraft in RAFG. It can carry a full range of air-to-surface weapons in its bomb-bay and on underwing pylons and is particularly suited to the deeper interdiction and counter-air roles.

'Deeper interdiction' usually refers to missions similar to those undertaken by the Jaguar, but further behind the battle region against troop concentrations, supply areas, headquarters and similar targets whose destruction would have a rapid impact on the land battle itself. The navigation, target acquisition and electronic countermeasure equipment carried by Buccaneer makes it a powerful all-weather conventional bomber. Converted to its nuclear strike role, it extends the flexibility of the response of options open to SACEUR.

In 'counter air' operations, the Buccaneer's contribution to the land battle would be less obvious, but perhaps even more significant. There is little doubt that a Warsaw Pact offensive would be accompanied by large scale air attack, not only on our airfields, but against our own troops, armour, reinforcement routes, headquarters and supplies. It is, therefore, imperative that such an air offensive be checked. Clearly, a heavy toll would be exacted by Allied interceptors and surface-to-air defences, but offensive air action is essential to disrupt the Warsaw Pact air armies at their source, otherwise the enemy would retain an initiative which history has proved time and again to be extremely dangerous to one who concedes it. Buccaneer numbers were depleted in 1980 when a fatigue crack was discovered in an inner main spar bracket but, by the beginning of 1981, a large proportion of the force was returned to Service after remedial action had been taken.

Fortunately, there were no longer-term implications of the depletion because, in 1983, the Buccaneers of XV and 16 Squadrons will be replaced by Tornado GR1. If the current squadron indentities are preserved, two more proud traditions will have continued. No 15 Squadron, known by its Roman

Right: A Buccaneer of No XV Squadron from Laarbruch displays its voluminous bomb bay over the low lying North German plain.

numerals 'XV' was formed in 1915, under Major (later Air Chief Marshal Sir Philip) Joubert de la Ferté. Since then, it has almost always been a bomber squadron, flying Blenheims, Stirlings and Lancasters. No 16 Squadron was formed in February 1915 at St Omer — hence its nickname of 'The Saints' — and until 1958 flew Army co-operation fighter and ground attack aircraft. Until it re-equipped with Buccaneers in 1972, it was the last Royal Air Force front-line squadron to fly Canberra bombers. In 1983, it may become one of the first to be equipped with Tornado GR1.

The advent of Tornado will considerably enhance the offensive strength of the Royal Air Force generally, but it will have a particular significance in RAFG. Its inertial navigation system, automatic terrain following ability, target acquisition equipment and electronic counter-measures fit will allow it to deliver weapons with many times the accuracy of any previous RAF strike/attack aircraft, in all weathers through the most concentrated enemy air defences. Consequently, the threat to enemy formations, reinforcements and airfields will be greatly increased. Moreover, possession of internal power and internal starter will considerably reduce turn-round times and facilitate cross-servicing when Tornado lands away from its own base. Its shorter take-off ability will help it to operate from damaged runways and to recover to autobahns and other emergency strips. It will be able to carry all the existing generation of RAF air-to-surface weapons, plus the specialist anti-armour and delayed action munition specified in the Air Staff Requirement 1227. In the counter-air role it will deliver JP 233, the combined runway cratering and area denial weapon designed for use against Warsaw Pact airfields. The Tornado GR1 has the potential for considerable further development and it is not impossible that the Laarbruch squadrons may ultimately be capable of delivering stand-off 'cruise' missiles which themselves could disperse sub-munitions against ground forces or airfields. Moreover, when both Italian and German Air Forces also equip with Tornado, interoperation between the Allies will be greatly increased. In short, the advent of Tornado to Laarbruch and elsewhere in

RAFG will mark the biggest improvement in British airpower in the region since World War 2.

But, even Tornado has to know where its targets are and, in the case of a fast-moving conflict, the need for swift, flexible and long range reconnaissance vehicles will remain. At present, that need is filled by the third squadron operating from Laarbruch, No 2, whose Jaguars carry a specially designed reconnaissance pod on the centre line position. The pod contains F-95 cameras and infra-red line scan equipment synchronised with the aircrafts' NAVWASS. The infra-red photography defeats normal camouflage by registering the heat impressions of the vehicles, aircraft, buildings and, indeed, any other reason for temperature differentials on the ground within its focal range. No 2 Squadron was formed in 1912 at Farnborough and in the person of Second Lieutenant W. B. Rhodes Moorhouse gained the Royal Flying Corps its first VC for aerial combat in April 1915. Since 1939, the Squadron has operated almost entirely in the photo-reconnaissance role. It could be replaced during the next decade by the fighter-reconnaissance variant of the Tornado GR-1, thereby further demonstrating the logistic and support advantages of the deployment of a multi-role aircraft, quite apart from the increased operational capability inherent in it.

Off-Base Operations

As Tornado begins to enter service at Laarbruch, a very different kind of aircraft will continue to operate from the fourth flying station in RAFG. Gutersloh, the only RAFG airfield to be located east of the Rhine, just 80 miles from the nearest section of the

Below: Field deployment of Harriers in May 1981. Operating from metal strips and roads for short take-offs and living in well camouflaged hides, the Harrier's unique V/STOL capability makes it a potent force that the Warsaw Pact would have no guarantee of knocking out in a pre-emptive strike.

inner German Border, is the home of Nos 3 and 4 Harrier Squadrons and No 230, equipped with Puma helicopters. No 3 Squadron was actually formed before the Royal Flying Corps as it flew as No 2 (Aeroplane) Company of the Air Battalion of the Royal Engineers in 1911. During its renowned fighter and ground attack history it shot down 288 pilotless V-1 aircraft over England in the later stages of World War 2 prior to becoming part of Second Tactical Air Force. Thereafter, it has served in Germany, converting to Harriers at Wildenrath in 1971 and moving to Gutersloh in 1977 when Gutersloh and Wildenrath exchanged roles and aircraft. No 4 Squadron was formed in 1912, a few months after No 3 and has, for most of its history, distinguished itself in the fighter-ground attack and fighter reconnaissance roles. In August 1970, it became the first squadron to operate fixed wing V/STOL jet fighters outside Britain when it re-equipped with the Harrier GR Mk 1 at Wildenrath. With No 3 Squadron, it also moved to Gutersloh in 1977. By 1980, both Squadrons were flying the GR Mk 3 and the two-seat T Mk 4.

Harrier is powered by a single Rolls-Royce Pegasus vectored thrust turbo-fan jet engine, which by means of two pairs of rotatable nozzles can vector the exhaust gases from 20% forward of the vertical to horizontally aft. This configuration allows the aircraft not only to land and to take-off vertically, but by varying the vector in flight it can decelerate extremely rapidly and attain a very high degree of manoeuvrability. Such a combination makes the Harrier a difficult and dangerous target for fighters which theoretically have far superior performance. It has a maximum level flight speed of about Mach 0.95 and is supersonic in a shallow dive. It has a radius of action of 450 miles and its ferry or operational ranges may be extended by in-flight refuelling. It can carry 5,000lb of weapons on seven external points which could include SNEB rockets, Aden 30mm cannon in wing pods, free-fall or retarded bombs, but its usual weapon load is the 600lb BL-755 cluster bomb which distributes a pattern of sub-munitions lethal to ground forces over a wide area.

It is, however, not its weapon load but its method of operation which makes the Harrier unique in European airpower. In a period of rising tension, Wildenrath, Laarbruch and Bruggen would seem deserted, with their Phantoms, Tornados and Jaguars securely protected in their closed HAS. But Gutersloh might really be deserted, at least by the Harrier Force which would literally have gone to ground, scattered among the woods, barns and even villages of the surrounding countryside close to the ground forces of No 1 (British) Corps of the Allied Northern Army Group with whom Nos 3 and 4 Squadrons would co-operate. In peacetime, of course, the Harriers disperse well away from farms and villages, but in war every location offering cover from hostile reconnaissance and a space for a short take off and vertical recovery would be potentially a Harrier air base.

Peacetime training for the Harrier Force, therefore, presents all the airborne challenges met by more conventional aircraft plus the need for mastery of the VTOL techniques and the task of locating, preparing and operating from remote sites. Not only must the aircraft be well hidden, but space must be found for fuel, weapons, signals and living complexes essential to the support of the Harriers in the field. Sometimes grass or woodland clearings need to be strengthened by steel strips but in a real emergency much greater use would be made of country lanes and roads. When the site is fully prepared, and the Harriers are at stand-by in them, they are virtually invisible to ordinary aerial reconnaissance although infra-red line-scan equipped aircraft would pick them out, if they were flying in the right area in the first place.

At war, the Harrier crews in their cockpits would await the telebrief from squadron or site operations, passed by secure channel from the joint Army-Support Operation Centre. They would have received continual intelligence up-dates giving the positions of both sides now locked in combat on the ground. Prefixed by the individual aircraft call-sign the 'immediate'

request would tersely describe the target: 'armour at such-and-such a grid reference', or 'line search on road a, b, c'. The pilot might then swiftly enter the appropriate co-ordinates in his inertial navigation attack system or, more likely, simply check his maps for a point which he would almost certainly know off by heart after many hours of flying over the ground, and prepare to move out. Camouflage net would be thrown back, the Harrier would move out from the trees, turn down the lane or field and be airborne in a very few seconds. Transiting at perhaps 150ft, with four cluster weapons, the pilot might be given a target up-date by the forward air controller down below with the ground forces. In a fast-moving battle, it is obviously essential that the pilot should receive the most accurate and up-to-date information. Taking advantage of his high speed and knowledge of the terrain to fly at very low altitude, he would take the forward air defences by surprise and be over his target less than 20 minutes after the request for his assistance had been made. With the cluster bomb units he has no need to climb to make a shallow dive attack; simply one fast pass and a large area of ground is spattered with bomblets able to severely damage all kinds of ground vehicles. Then, back to the puma, still at very low level, perhaps using the differential vector thrust to evade enemy interception. Each aircraft or pilot could be expected to fly up to five such missions a day providing considerable assistance to hard-pressed, probably outnumbered, ground forces.

The Harrier concept of operations is, therefore, quite unique. On the one hand, forward deployment permits very fast reaction to requests for assistance to ground forces. But also, should the Warsaw Pact ever contemplate a pre-emptive attack on NATO's airpower, they would be aware that they would have no guarantee of knocking out, or even grounding the Harrier force. Indeed, they would have no idea where to look for it. So the ability to operate from dispersed sites is not just of offensive value, but by reducing the aircraft's vulnerability and by complicating the Warsaw Pact's own offensive calculations, the Harrier force clearly makes a powerful contribution to deterrence.

Moreover, that contribution will be further increased during the next decade. It is likely that the current aircraft will be fitted with AIM-9L Sidewinder air-to-air missiles which would make Harrier an even more difficult opponent and with radar and infra-red surface-to-air defence suppression equipment. In the longer term, the Gutersloh squadrons will be equipped, like No 1 Squadron at Wittering, with the McDonnell Douglas AV-8B with subsequent development of a supersonic 'super Harrier'.

The Helicopter Force

The other permanent resident at Gutersloh in 1981, No 230 Puma Squadron, is equally unlikely to be at home should Frontal Aviation call. Its function is to provide tactical transport and battlefield support facilities for No 1 (British) Corps and, like the Harriers during a period of tension, it would deploy off base. Unlike its fixed wing colleagues, No 230 Squadron originated in naval aviation, as part of the Royal Naval Air Service War Flight based at Felixstowe in World War 1. It became No 230 Squadron in 1918 and until 1957 had a distinguished maritime record which included support to Wingate's Chindits by flying to the Brahmaputra River and, after World War 2, contributing to the Berlin Airlift by flights to Lake Havel. It arrived at Gutersloh with its Pumas in late 1980.

The SA-330 Puma Mk 1 is a joint product of SNAIS and Westlands. It is powered by two Turbomeca 111 C4 engines of 130shp each and can carry 16 troops or internal and external loads of up to 2,500kg. It has a maximum range of 390 miles and a cruising speed of 165mph.

In peacetime, Pumas deploy for exercises in small numbers under camouflage in woods and near farm buildings from where they can swiftly provide logistic support, troop mobility, casualty evacuation or with side-mounted machine guns they can operate as gunships. They are accompanied by an army officer who would

usually be an Army Air Corps pilot and a logistic expert who would act as a link between the Squadron and No 1 (British) Corps.

In 1982, the Puma Squadron will be joined by the Boeing Chinook HC-1s of No 18 Squadron which will have previously reformed at Odiham. Of particular value in RAFG will be Chinook's wide tolerance of extreme temperatures from 32°C to +52°C, quite apart from its year-round all-weather capability by day and night. The fact that it can carry 44 fully equipped troops, or a variety of heavy loads such as a five-ton truck or a bridge section or total payload of 21,000lb 250 miles will add considerably to the air mobility of the land and air forces east of the Rhine. The timely and swift deployment of men and equipment to reinforce, to manoeuvre and to regroup will be a vital attribute in the fast-moving warfare which would be likely in the Central Region.

The Posture

Although flying very different kinds of aircraft, the pilots of Gutersloh are manifestly in the same team as their colleagues at Bruggen, Wildenrath, Laarbruch and back at Headquarters at Rheindahlen. All are aware that they could receive little warning of impending conflict; all are aware that they must not only be prepared to survive an initial blow, but to be able to counter attack to such effect that with their Army colleagues they would be able to halt an invader long before he had achieved his objectives. The constant state of readiness maintained by Royal Air Force Germany, which is no doubt perceived from across the Inner German Border, is a strong guarantor of continued peace and stability in the Central Region.

Below: No 230 Squadron provides tactical transport and battlefield support facilities for 1(BR) Corps in West Germany. Employing the SA-330 Puma — here one is seen near a well-known landmark near Detmold, the Hermannsdenkmal — the squadron will be joined in 1982 by the Chinooks of No 18 Squadron.

Jaguars in Germany

Low level sorties are routine for the Jaguars of No 31 Squadron — but in time of war they would be lower still!

Right: The eyes and ears of the offensive support squadrons. A Jaguar of No 2 Squadron at Laarbruch on a training photo-reconnaissance sortie.

Below right: A tight formation for Jaguars of No 20 Squadron.

NATO co-operation

Above: A Jaguar of No 31 Squadron, RAF Bruggen leads a Canadian Armed Force F-104 of No 421 Squadron to the exercise area in North Germany. Joint exercises and sorties are practised continually in RAFG as evinced by these two photographs (left) of a No 17 Squadron Jaguar and a Luftwaffe F-104 simulated attack sortie from Bruggen. There are also frequent exchange missions and, for example, (above right) No 2 Squadron, RAF Laarbruch hosted No 42 Squadron of the Belgian Air Force in Novemeber 1980 — here a Jaguar and Mirage sit on the hardstand.

Right: A Jaguar T2 of No 2 Squadron returns to its HAS at Laarbruch after a sortie.

Exercise 'Mini Val'

A tactical exercise designed to evaluate the working efficiency of a station while under attack, Exercise 'Mini Val' was held in August 1976. Here (this page) a 1,000lb bomb is prepared for loading and attached to a Jaguar's underwing pylon by groundcrew working under NBC conditions. Right: Also in the NBC kit are the air traffic controllers and (below right) ambulancemen evacuating a 'casualty' during the exercise.

Buccaneers

Above and right: A Buccaneer of No 16 Squadron moves out of its HAS towards the main runway during an exercise at Laarbruch. Note folded wings — a reminder of the Buccaneer's Fleet Air Arm service.

Below right: Buccaneer S Mk 2 of No 16 Squadron.

In time of war ground maintenance of both aircraft and airfields is of major importance. Left: RAF groundcrews have consistently won international competitions for speedy turn rounds of strike and attack aircraft. Here their PR colleagues demonstrate similar skills for No 2 Squadron at Laarbruch. Below: Sappers from Waterbeach demonstrate the value of their runway repair equipment at Wildenrath.

Dispersed Operations

The Harrier's unique operating capabilities allow a relative freedom from a pre-emptive strike. Here Harriers of No 3 Squadron (above) and No 4 Squadron (left) prepare for sorties from dispersed sites. Of course, not only the aircraft and their crews have to operate in such situations — (above right) Forward Wing Operations Control, based for mobility in caravans, directs the Harriers to their targets and (right) groundcrew perform the necessary maintenance (here an engine change for a No 3 Squadron Harrier) in the field.

A rare sight was seen at the USAF base of Bitburg in December 1980 when F-15 Eagle pilots of the 525th TFS hosted Jaguar crews of No 20 Squadron. Left: Major Bob Jessup, USAF makes a point for the benefit of the crews, and (below) a Jaguar and an F-15 on a wintry airfield.

Bottom: The inauguration of a major NATO exercise — 'Autumn Forge' — at RAF Gutersloh on 8 September 1980. Air Marshal Sir Peter Terry, Commander of the Second Allied Tactical Air Force and Commander-in-Chief Royal Air Force Germany, 'meets the troops' of the nations taking part. Here he is talking to Private Gerry Speight of the 21st Cavalry from Fort Hood, Texas.

Right: No 4 Squadron Harriers in flight showing the difference between the GR3's laser rangefinder nose (above) and the original GR1 configuration.

Above: Winter Survival — a Puma of No 230 Squadron 'rescues' a student from a Winter Survival School.

Centre right: A Wessex of No 18 squadron providing battlefield mobility for troops on exercise in Germany.

Bottom right: The imposing castle of Neuschwanstein provides a backdrop for a Wessex V helicopter of No 18 Squadron, based at RAF Gutersloh, gaining experience in the mountainous terrain of Bavaria away from the flat plains of Northern Germany.

7

Air Mobility

Should a crisis ever occur in Europe, Royal Air Force Germany would not be left to fight a war on its own, nor would Allied armies be left unreinforced. In September 1980, a massive NATO exercise was mounted to test the ability of the Alliance to move men and supplies swiftly into Central Europe. RAF Gutersloh was one of the reception airfields and in three days accepted 55 sorties by Boeing 737s, 747s, VC-10s, Tri-Stars, BAC-111s and Hercules. In all, 20,000 British Territorial soldiers were moved to the Continent in a few hours, and a very large proportion of them by air. On this occasion, Royal Air Force transport aircraft were augmented by civilian airlines as they would be in a real crisis. But, in peacetime, round the clock all year round, the air support squadrons of the Royal Air Force considerably increase the flexibility and reach of ground forces by giving them both tactical and strategic air mobility.

The heart of the Royal Air Force's Tactical Transport Force is at Royal Air Force Lyneham in Wiltshire, the home of the Hercules fleet. The Hercules entered RAF service in 1967, replacing the Hastings and Beverley. It shows every sign of becoming the Dakota of the 1980s because of its astonishing versatility. Although it has a 4,600 mile range with a 20,000lb payload and cruises at 345mph, it can also operate comfortably from short unprepared strips. Its rugged construction and high serviceability rate makes it an excellent tactical transport. The C Mk1 is similar to the Hercules C-130E used by the USAF but the four by 4,910eshp Allison turbo-prop engines are rather more powerful than those in the 130E. It can carry 92 fully armed troops or a variety of vehicles: three Ferret Scout cars plus 30 troops or two Scout helicopters or a Saladin armoured car plus a Ferret. In parachute dropping, its roller conveyor system facilitates the despatch of heavy platforms in excess of 30,000lb. Sixty-two paratroops can be dropped from the fuselage side-doors or 40 from the rear load ramp. When used for casualty evacuation, it can carry 74 stretchers.

The major units at Lyneham are No 242 OCU and Nos 24, 30, 47 and 70 Squadrons. 242 OCU is responsible for the training of all five aircrew members of the Hercules: the two pilots, navigator, air engineer and air loadmaster. The complete course lasts for five months comprising ground school, simulator and flying phases. The co-pilot, for example, would fly some 20 hours general handling and instrumental flying plus another 36 on 'route' training. A further 36 hours would be spent by the entire converting crew in one of three simulators which can reproduce a range of situations from emergency drills to approaches into difficult airfields, such as Katmandu in Nepal.

On successfully 'converting' to the Hercules, the crew members join one of the four operational squadrons. All have long and distinguished records as transport units but now discharge slightly differing roles. No 24, which was formed as a fighter squadron in 1915 has flown all the RAF's major transport aircraft since 1920 and No 30, which was expressly formed for overseas service in 1914 but flew fighter operations in World war 2 before becoming a transport squadron in 1947, undertake route flying tasks only. Nos 47, a transport squadron which flew in the Berlin Airlift and which has flown Hercules since 1968, and 70, which dropped paratroops on Port Said in 1956 during a 55-year unbroken period of service in the Middle East, also have transport support tasks. These include low level operations by day and night, dropping men and equipment by parachute and airborne assault techniques. Before crews undertake these roles, they must return to the OCU for a further specialised three-week course. Thereafter, they will work with the parachute battalions of the British Army, both in day-to-day training and in airborne assault exercises which take place annually in the United Kingdom and NATO-wide in Europe. Such exercises may be straightforward missions in which a stream of Hercules would fly direct to a dropping zone (DZ) or they may, on the other hand, call for low level diversionary routeing through or around simulated air-to-air or ground-to-air defences. Carefully selected crews may be tasked to work with units of the Special Air Service or the Special Boat Service of the Royal Marines. Such air support is the descendant of the work in World War 2 with special operations forces and clearly calls for the highest navigational and flying skills in a variety of demanding environments worldwide.

The Hercules Force, as a whole, has three major tasks: support of NATO, support of national commitments and assistance to other nations. NATO operations could include the support of the ACE Mobile Force or the UK Mobile Force on its deployment to the mainland of Europe. In peacetime, it will involve participation in major NATO exercises, such as Crusader 80, which took place on the North German Plain in September 1980. 102,000 troops and supporting equipment were involved in a test of British ability to mobilise and to reinforce swiftly the British Army of the Rhine. The Lyneham Hercules were inevitably heavily involved. In the passenger fit they flew troops into the airhead at Gutersloh and supported the deployment of Nos 1, 54 and 72 Squadrons from the United Kingdom to forward bases. In the Transport Support role, they dropped 300 paratroops directly into the combat zone, near the Weser Canal, simulating a hostile diversionary brigade. Such activities, albeit on a smaller scale, comprise the first priority for the Hercules Force all the year round.

The second priority, of supporting British national commitments, includes the regular support of our forces in Belize and Northern Ireland. Occasionally, however, a major national task arises such as the evacuation of British subjects from Cyprus in 1974 or from Iran in 1979. But, by far the most significant task was the mounting of Exercise 'Agila' in December 1979 and January 1980: the use of airpower to facilitate the progress of Rhodesia to independence.

After the Lancaster House agreements of 1979, it was essential that the Commonwealth Monitoring Force should be swiftly

The Hercules has been with the RAF since 1967 and recently celebrated its 500,000th flying hour in service. To commemorate the occasion a flypast was made at RAF Lyneham, heart of the RAF's transport force. Left: Birds' eye view of the formation from the fourth aircraft; and (above) the representatives of Lyneham's four squadrons overfly a trumpeter of the Junior Leaders' Band, RCT.

deployed and that the Patriotic Front Guerillas should be adequately supplied in their new Assembly Areas. The Hercules mounted over 250 sorties, lifting 5,000 passengers and over $2\frac{1}{2}$ million pounds of freight of which three quarters of a million were air-dropped because no other means of resupply was feasible. The tactical support sorties were flown by crews from Nos 47 and 70 Squadrons. The weather was frequently poor, with rain, poor visibility and cloud base of 2-300ft. Moreover, there was, from the outset, the possibility that Patriotic Front Guerillas would use their SAM-7s, RPG-7 rocket launchers or 7.62 machine guns against the Hercules. In the event, one Hercules did take a 7.62 round which narrowly missed the liquid oxygen supply and all flying had to be planned on the assumption of a hostile threat from the ground. Transit speeds were in the order of 260kts indicated air speed at below 200ft. Airdrops were made into clearings as small as half a football field and often surrounded by trees, minefields, rocks and other obstacles. Some of the Hercules had their undercarriages strengthened to facilitate short, unmade strip landings and take-offs which quickly became commonplace in the exercise. Navigation was made more difficult by the need to improvise maps and charts and by the scarcity of prominent features in unfamiliar terrain, but the Commonwealth Monitoring Force was deployed within the three days which had been requested and the Patriotic Front Guerilla assembly areas were all re-supplied even though on occasions the Hercules were flying five sorties a day in very bad weather. The extremely high standards of efficiency in the Hercules fleet were amply demonstrated.

Later in 1980, a third priority task of the fleet, that of giving assistance to other countries, arose when a Hercules of No 70 Squadron was detached to Katmandu to drop over 1,000 tons of rice and wheat to starving villagers in the mountains of Nepal. In operation 'Khana Cascade 80' the Hercules flew the supplies to three remote dropping zones 8,000ft up in the mountain valleys

103

below low clouds which heralded the onset of the monsoon. Without the airdrop the villagers were facing starvation after the failure of their own crops.

Exercises such as 'Crusader', 'Agila', or 'Khana Cascade' obviously call for meticulous planning but the Hercules fleet also maintains a 24-hour all-year-round quick readiness alert (QRA) posture in order to react to emergency or crises anywhere in the world. Moreover, ability to respond to such crisis will be increased in the immediate future by the stretching of the fuselage of 30 Hercules to increase their carrying capacity. The programme will be completed by late 1983 and will have the operational effect of adding eight aircraft to the fleet.

The Support Helicopter Force

But if the backbone of the RAF's 'air mobility' may be said to be the Hercules, because of its payload and long reach, it has a considerable complement in the Support Helicopter Force which has its headquarters at RAF Odiham in Hampshire. Until 1981, No 240 OCU was responsible for converting all crews to both Wessex and Puma helicopters but, as the result of Chinook coming into service, the Wessex training was transferred to Royal Air Force Benson, together with Nos 72 and 18 Wessex Squadrons.

The main functions of the Support Helicopter Force are to provide battlefield mobility of troops and supplies and to support the Harrier forward deployments. No 33 Squadron operates Pumas at Odiham and was accompanied in that role by No 230 Squadron until the latter moved to Gutersloh in 1980. In addition to contributing to NATO exercises in the United Kingdom and on the mainland of Europe, the Helicopter Force also has purely national commitments. One detachment of Pumas is permanently deployed to Belize while another works with the security forces in Northern Ireland. The ability of the Puma to carry loads of up to 5,500lb as underslung cargo is of great value to the security forces. In addition to providing mobility for 16 fully equipped troops, it can lift vehicles, provisions or even a mundane concrete mixer from point to point, thereby denying terrorists a relatively soft target on the remote winding lanes near the border in South Armagh.

The Puma Force also contributed to Exercise 'Agila'. Six Pumas were airlifted by United States Air Force C-5A 'Galaxy' transport to Rhodesia and, while the Hercules were tasked with the heavy duties, the helicopters carried out the lighter air supply tasks, casualty evacuation and ferrying passengers between Salisbury and the various Patriotic Front assembly areas. In the four months of the detachment, the six helicopters flew 848 hours, carrying over 160,000lb of freight and 3,000 passengers. Despite the unfamiliar geographical conditions, the Pumas maintained a 97% serviceability rate throughout all sorties.

Although only the Pumas were deployed to Rhodesia, the longer serving Wessex participated in Exercise 'Crusader 80', bears the brunt of the detachment in Northern Ireland and continues to provide tactical mobility to the British Army, both within NATO and in Hong Kong. Indeed, in 1981, the rotational detachment of helicopters from Odiham to Northern Ireland was replaced by the permanent positioning of No 72 Squadron. Although lacking the lifting power of the Puma, the twin-engined Wessex has a longer range and can carry seven stretchers, 15 troops or 3,600lb of freight and will continue to make a valuable contribution to tactical mobility for some time.

In the immediate future, however, that tactical mobility will be considerably enhanced by the entry into service of the Boeing

Below: While the Hercules may be said to be the basis of the RAF's doctrine of air mobility, the Support Helicopter Force based at RAF Odiham certainly complements the heavyweight transport aircraft. Here a Puma of No 230 Squadron (which in 1980 moved to Gutersloh, RAFG) is seen on a casualty exercise near Odiham.

Chinook HC-1 heavy-lift helicopters. Thirty-three Chinooks have been ordered for the Royal Air Force and the first arrived at Odiham to begin the Chinook Flight of No 240 OCU in December 1980. The first squadron was training at Odiham during 1981 and will deploy to Germany during 1982, to supplement the Pumas at Gutersloh. The second squadron will be based in the United Kingdom, probably at Odiham, and will add to the tactical mobility of the ACE and United Kingdom Mobile Forces.

A mere list of Chinook's vital statistics do not convey the dramatic increase in capability which the new Force will confer. The helicopters will be able to carry over 20,000lb payload at a maximum speed of 175kts and will have a range of 250 miles. It has three cargo hooks to allow it to deliver three separate underslung loads to different destinations and its interior cabin is 30ft long, 8ft 3in wide and 6ft 6in high. It can land on water and remain afloat at sea-state two for at least two hours when still weighing 36,000lb gross. But, in practical terms, these figures mean that Chinook could recover an unserviceable Harrier, or move 44 fully armed troops, or ten tons of ammunition or fuel, or a five-ton truck in all weathers by day or night, over a combat radius which covers all the territory under the wing of RAF Germany. Expressed another way, that is a range and payload combination almost four times greater than that of Puma. With internal long range fuel tanks its ferry range can be increased to 1,000 miles, conveying even greater flexibility for out of theatre deployment. In due course, all the RAF's Chinooks will be fitted with glass-fibre blades to increase reliability, facilitate servicing and make the aircraft more resistant to battle damage. Needless to say, the full operational deployment of Chinook is enthusiastically welcomed by both the RAF and the NATO allies.

Strategic Mobility

As the tactical demands on air mobility have increased over the last decade with the concentration of the United Kingdom's defence effort on Europe, so the requirement for long range strategic airlift has declined. Consequently, the Short Belfasts and the Bristol Britannias were withdrawn from service, leaving the VC-10s of No 10 Squadron to discharge the long range rapid reinforcement task in addition to the Hercules in their strategic configuration. Thirteen of the 14 C Mk 1s which entered service with No 10 Squadron in 1967 will continue operations well beyond the next decade. The 14th was used by Rolls-Royce as a flying testbed for the RB-211 engine and was honourably grounded in 1976.

The VC-10 can carry 150 troops or up to 78 stretcher cases or 54,000lb of freight which could be distributed between the upper cabin and two large lower freight holds. The load could comprise five Scout cars or five Landrovers and trailers which could be carried over a range of 3,700 miles at about 565mph. It is interesting to observe that although the original United Kingdom presence in the Middle and Far East which prompted the procurement of the VC-10 has now largely disappeared, the public statements of Mrs Thatcher in March 1981 about an Allied 'presence' beyond NATO's specified boundaries suggest that the VC-10 may revert to its distinguished primary role of earlier days. Until it does, its range will continue to permit its shuttle use within Europe as was done in Exercise 'Crusader' when it flew between Brize Norton and Gutersloh, moving auxiliary forces into BAOR.

Below: The Boeing Chinook HC-1 will considerably enhance the tactical mobility of the RAF. Here the first Chinook for the RAF is seen at the handover ceremony at Boeing Vertol's Philidelphia plant in April 1980.

The Queen's Flight

The VC-10 may also be called upon to carry members of the Royal Family on long range overseas visits, but the regular transport of Her Majesty and the Royal Family is the very special responsibility of the Queen's Flight at Royal Air Force Benson in Oxfordshire. The Flight comprises three Hawker Siddeley Andover CC-2s and two Wessex HCC-4s. The Andover, which joined the Queen's Flight in 1964 is a development of the commercial Hawker Siddeley 748 short range airliner, which it closely resembles. It has a shorter fuselage than the standard service short range transport and is used solely for VIP flying. The Queen's Flight aircraft is modified to include special interior layout and extra communications equipment.

In 1979, the Andovers flew 1,581 hours of which 1,033 were for training, route proving or positioning. Of the others, 433 hours involved the carriage of members of the Royal Family and 115 hours involved Ministers and other VIPs. The Andovers are employed for longer journeys up to 800 miles and the Wessex for short journeys up to 200 miles. For ranges longer than 800 miles, either the VC-10 or civilian aircraft are used. It is a proud boast by the Queens Flight that it has not lost a trip in over a decade and that since the arrival of the Wessex and Andovers, 'Doors Open' has very seldom been delayed more than a couple of minutes. Such reliability, however, does not arise by accident but is the product of meticulous, dedicated teamwork by the aircrew and groundcrew of the Flight.

The entire Queen's Flight is run by less than 200 people. Until 1981, the Captain was Air Commodore Archie Winskill CVO, CBE, DFC who was a retired RAF officer and a member of the Royal Household. The chain of command in the Royal Air Force passes through AOC 38 Group to Headquarters Strike Command. The groundcrew work a nominal three-shift system but, in fact, they work until the required aircraft are serviceable. Every flight must be 100% serviceable, helicopter ground runs must be completed one and a half hours before departure and aircraft are always prepositioned one and a half hours before requirement with, if bad weather should threaten, overnight predeployment. Additional engine life safety factors are employed. For example, the Wessex Gnome engine is changed after 1,000 hours rather than 1,200 hours on the squadrons and the rotor gearbox after 600 hours rather than the standard 800. All flight engineers and pilots are on five-year postings and, although discipline is strict throughout the Flight and standards are the highest, there is never any shortage of aircrew or groundcrew willing to serve in such a responsible and prestigious area.

The question of replacing the Andovers has been raised on several occasions in Parliament since the Air Force Board in 1972 approved an order for two BAC-111 jets; an order which was rejected by the government of the day. In March 1980, Mr Pattie, Under Secretary of State for the Royal Air Force, said in the House of Commons that there were no immediate plans to replace the Andover but that no final decision had been made. He suggested that on the one hand the Andover was an excellent short field aircraft, but on the other it did not have a long distance range akin to that of the VC-10. Certainly, it could be expected that a replacement aircraft would be welcomed by all those concerned with flight planning. Excellent an aeroplane as the Andover undoubtedly is, a jet airliner of the capability of the BAC-111 would reduce airway time, reduce the number of intermediate stops and, consequently, ease flight planning complications and reduce opportunities for security incidents. But as Mr Pattie concluded, 'I have no doubt that whatever the outcome of the study (into replacements) the Queen's Flight will continue to provide the excellent service that it has done to date'.

Air Mobility

Taken together, the VC-10s, Hercules, helicopters and other transport aircraft of 38 Group add the irreplaceable elements of high speed and extended range to British and Allied ground forces. The Queen's Flight and every other squadron in the Air Transport Force have a safety and reliability record second to none. Operations such as 'Agila', 'Khana Cascade' and 'Crusader' have shown that they confer a degree of mobility to support national policy unmatched by any NATO ally other than the United States of America.

Below: The sleek lines of a VC-10 of No 10 Squadron with 'everything down' on a slow flypast over RAF Abingdon.

Hercules

The Lockheed C 130 Hercules has been one of the most successful postwar multi-purpose transport aircraft. It first flew in 1954 and entered RAF service in 1967. A versatile and rugged aircraft it is primarily intended for tactical operations, but has recently been used for mercy missions around the world as can be seen later in this section. As a troop carrier, the Hercules can carry 92 fully armed men and for airborne operations 62 paratroopers can be despatched in two simultaneous sticks from the fuselage side doors. Freight loads can be parachuted from the larger rear doors of the aircraft — up to a weight of 30,000lb. Among other heavyweight military loads which can be carried are: three Ferret scout cars plus 30 passengers; two Scout helicopters; or a Saladin armoured car plus Land Rover or Ferret.

Above: Hercules of the Lyneham Wing.

Left: Paradrop: here on to the relatively wide open spaces of Salisbury Plain — tomorrow the same Hercules from No 47 Squadron could be en route to the Himalayan valleys of Nepal.

Left: Two more views of C1s from the Lyneham Wing.

Above: The first 'stretched' Hercules, designated the C Mk 3, was delivered to the RAF on 8 August 1980. It has been lengthened by 15ft (8ft 4in forward of the wings and 6ft 8in aft) and is shown dropping a 7ton load on a cluster of three parachutes.

Centre right: A Land Rover is unloaded from an RAF Hercules at Karup Air Force Base, Denmark at the start of a two-week exercise.

Bottom right: Dense cargo for a Hercules of the Lyneham Wing.

Pre-Flight Preparation

Above: Flight planning documents are issued to the pilot of a Hercules crew . . . who then gets to work with his crew in the ops centre.

Right: Final checks on the flightdeck — captain, pilot and flight engineer, and down the back (below right) the Airloadmaster.

Mercy Missions

This page: Scenes at Don Muang Airport, Bangkok, as a Hercules of No 24 Squadron loads cartons of cooking oil, a highly ornate 2½ton Izusu truck and sacks of rice, all of which will be flown to Cambodia as part of the Red Cross mission.

Exercise 'Agila' — (below) a trio of Hercules C1 aircraft from the Lyneham Wing at Salisbury International airport in December 1979; and (bottom) dropping supplies to an ex-guerilla assembly point in the bush.

VC10

Above: Passengers boarding VC10 *Guy Gibson VC* **of No 10 Squadron at its base at Brize Norton, Oxon.**

Left: As a VC10 trooper from Brize Norton offloads passengers at Akrotiri, Cyprus the catering groundcrew begin to prepare for the aircraft's return to the UK.

Nursing sisters of the Princess Mary's Royal
Nursing Service (above) on a preflight briefing
before a No 10 Squadron VC10 casevac flight
and (right) inside a VC10 configured for casualty
evacuation.

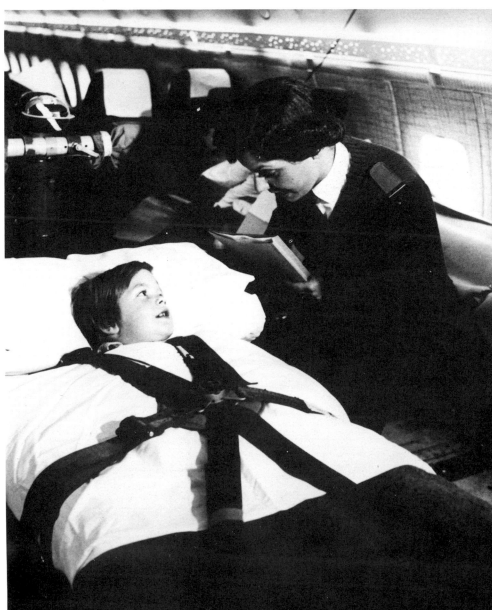

Support Helicopter Force

Above: A Puma taking part in Exercise 'Amber Express' in Denmark, September 1981.

Left: A helping hand from big brother! Lifting an army Gazelle which made an unscheduled stop in Belfast after mechanical failure, an RAF Puma gives a clear indication of its usefulness.

Left: Lifting the Army! A Chinook of No 240 OCU makes off with a Saladin armoured car during training at RAF Odiham.

Above and right: No 18 Squadron, RAF Odiham receives its first Chinook, ZA683, in August 1981.

Bottom right: Doing a wheelie! Chinook ZA675 of No 240 OCU demonstrates its versatility at Odiham Families Day, July 1981.

Right: A Gazelle of No 32 Squadron at RAF Northolt which provides air mobility for RAF officers, members of the government and other VIPs.

Below: A Chinook of No 18 Squadron in Denmark for Exercise 'Amber Express', September 1981.

8

Supply and Equipment

The RAF's transport fleet VC-10s and Hercules have, all being well, a very long fatigue life expectancy which should see them ranging the world well into the 1990s. But already in 1980, studies had begun in the MOD to assess the likely military transport requirement for the end of the century and to prepare plans and concepts for designing equipment to meet it.

Deterrence permitting, it was possible to envisage a design and development phase of 10 years for any military aircraft followed by perhaps another 25 years' operational service. The implications of that become apparent if one imagines going to the office one day in December 1980 and leaving at teatime having finalised proposals for equipment which must still be fulfilling the RAF's needs in December 2015. Taking a step backwards, the Vulcan Force was beginning to be withdrawn from service by the end of 1981 after being designed in the late 1940s, while the Nimrod conceived in its earliest shape in the 1940s, looked like outlasting the VC-10. Tornado, designed in the 1960s, would still be the backbone of the RAF 30 years later. In the USA, the B-52 could boast a similar lifespan while several Soviet aircraft were entering their third decade of active service, even though many new types had joined them. Not surprisingly, therefore, the supply of equipment for air forces in general and for the Royal Air Force in particular is a very complex and lengthy business. Although the details of the procurement process may vary slightly in detail, the basic procedure is as follows.

First, the RAF staffs will study the likely operational environment in the period in which a weapon system is likely to be entering service. For example, when Tornado was being considered, an assessment was made of the likely European battle arena in the late 1970s. It was considered that a potential aggressor could be expected to have extensive surface-to-air defences but would nevertheless be dependent on his airfields to provide essential airpower and on extensive reinforcements to support a large scale armoured offensive which would continue to form the basis of his strategy. Moreover, he could be expected to mount continuous operations by day and night regardless of weather. Obviously, such a broad analysis would be refined by considerable detail from many sources, but from even such a simplified assessment, the genesis of Tornado can be seen. An aircraft was required which had to be able to penetrate heavy air defences in all weathers by day and by night to attack enemy airfields and to interdict his reinforcements. The implications of that requirement, in terms of range, avionics, weapon fits and structural demands are obviously considerable. Moreover, in Tornado's case, the needs of three countries were to be co-ordinated in the interests of cost-effectiveness per unit.

If the project is a national one, however, then the air staff construct a 'staff target' (AST) as a basic for further analysis and development. Under the direction of the Procurement Executive of the MOD, the scientific and technical implications of the AST are examined. In an era of rapidly evolving technology, some very

accurate assessments must be made. For example, if the aircraft will fly operationally in six years' time, what advances in avionics or weapons can be expected in that period? What, in short, is the state of the military aviation art now and how far can further developments be anticipated? Errors in analysis in one direction will produce an airframe which is obsolescent as it begins its flight trials, while in the other you will be trying to design equipment which will be outstripping available technology and therefore will be either too expensive or too unreliable to put into production. Thus, at the earliest point advice is sought from MOD research establishments about the best options to pursue to achieve the greatest possible effectiveness from the funds likely to be available in the long term costings.

Even the most cursory glance at the Tornado will indicate how extremely difficult such analysis must be. Not, as in the happy days of the Bristol Fighter, an airframe, an engine, guns and a few simple instruments. Requirements for airframe and engines, although much more complex, remain, but now: hydraulics, electrical circuits, computers, automated systems, radars, lasers, electronic warning sensors, in-flight refuelling equipment, optical devices and over and above all that, the actual weapons to be delivered. The translation of the AST into a specific weapon system requirement, then into a development aircraft and, finally, into a Tornado on 617 Squadron require specialist skills; many of which are focused on one internationally renowned base near Salisbury in Wiltshire.

Aeroplane and Armament Experimental Establishment

The Aeroplane and Armament Experimental Establishment (A&AEE) at Boscombe Down has a major responsibility for trials of equipment and sub-systems associated with RAF equipment not just about to enter into service, but in some cases several years after the in-service date. A&AEE has grown from a very small unit known as Experimental Flight CFS which was set up at the Central Flying School, Upavon in 1914. The Flight had a staff of three: one pilot and two scientists who were serving in the Royal Flying Corps. Its equipment consisted of two BE-2s and its terms of reference included the development of methods of dropping bombs, firing guns, taking photographs from aircraft and the development of methods of air-to-ground and air-to-air signalling. It gradually expanded and as the Testing Squadron RFC, moved to Martlesham Heath in 1917 where it remained until the outbreak of war in September 1939 when it moved to Boscombe Down.

Initial flying of a new aircraft is carried out by the manufacturer: for the Tornado for example, by British Aerospace at Warton in Lancashire or for the Nimrod at Woodford in Cheshire, but at a previously agreed point the aircraft is handed over to A&AEE. At Boscombe Down a carefully selected team of Service pilots, drawn from the Army and the Royal Navy as well as from the RAF will work alongside civilian colleagues from the

Procurement Executive to test every aspect of the performance of the aircraft and its sub-systems. One Division, for example, is responsible for the acceptance trials of navigation/attack and radio/radar installations in new military aircraft and of modification by new equipments into existing aircraft. Assessment of the performance of navigation/attack systems is complex, involving parallel activities of flight testing and computer modelling. The Division also evaluates new equipment and systems being considered for installation in future military aircraft and selected civil navigation systems. For this work it operates a number of highly instrumented laboratory aircraft including a modified Phantom, Comet 4 and Sea King. Another Division is responsible for the evaluation of aircraft armaments which demands mechanical and electrical engineering appraisals of weapons and their associated aircraft installations to establish safety and suitability for Service use. Flight trials are conducted to assess conditions of carriage, normal release and jettison of bombs and fuel tanks and of the carriage and firing of missiles, guns and rockets. Interoperability trials are conducted with weapons of other NATO nations and a wide variety of aircraft is used including Sea Harrier, Phantom, Jaguar, Tornado and Buccaneer. In due course, JP-233 will pass through equally rigorous trials before acceptance as the major first-generation anti-airfield weapon to be carried by Tornado.

But variable as Wiltshire weather can be, it cannot provide the extremes of temperature that the Harriers of No 1 Squadron, or the Jaguars of Nos 6 and 54 may have to face if rapidly deployed to an arctic winter or a Middle Eastern summer. An indispensable facility at Boscombe Down is, therefore, the Environmental Test Centre which can subject an entire aircraft and sub-systems to temperatures ranging from $-40°C$ to $+35°C$ and 100%

Research by the A&AEE

Above left: A Tornado takes off for a trials sortie with underwing stores.

Left: A Wessex hovers in a spray rig in Ottawa during icing trials.

Above: A&AEE was responsible for clearing the airdropping of loads from the Hercules C1. This photograph shows the initial stages of the drop of an 18,000lb load with a Harvard chase aircraft in the foreground.

Right: A Lynx undergoing tethered hovering tests under 'hot and high' conditions in California. (RAF test pilots at A&AEE fly in a wide variety of aircraft for all three Services — here the Royal Navy.)

Above: The open jet blower tunnel in full spate during an icing trial.

The Empire Test Pilot School

ETPS was established at Boscombe Down in 1943 and after one or two deployments has been settled there since 1967. Each year 22 students, of whom some 50% are normally from overseas, attend either the Fixed Wing (FW), Rotary Wing (RW) or Flight Test Engineer (FTE) course. The 300-hour groundschool programme includes aero systems, lectures from military and industrial specialists and visits to aircraft manufacturers and air shows. On average, two hours per day are devoted to the theoretical basis for each of the flying exercises, of which there are approximately 20 for both FW and RW. One of the course aims is for the pilot to understand the language of the scientist and engineer to allow him to discuss problems on an equal footing. He must also learn to be able to identify the aircraft problem areas and limitations, master test flying techniques and to communicate his findings by clear, oral and written reports.

His flying experience will be broadened on nine FW or five RW types including a Jaguar, Lightning, Hunter, Andover, Canberra Hawk, Sea King, Lynx and Gazelle. He will be required to assess handling characteristics such as stability and control assessment and specific exercises such as manoeuvre boundaries or flight envelope investigation. His performance exercises will include accurate measurememt of rates of climb, pressure air corrections and hover performance. The third group of activities, systems include autopilots, navigation and attack systems and flight simulators. In addition to the 'straightforward' flying of the aircraft already mentioned the student will handle a specially modified Bassett whose stability and control characteristics can be varied to simulate a wide range of aircraft types and handling qualities by an analogue computer which, connected to the right-hand controls, feeds signals direct to the control surfaces.

humidity. And, whether operating in Arctic, European or sub-tropical conditions, aircraft, armament and avionics systems must remain safe and serviceable in varying electro-magnetic conditions. These are tested by installations which can simulate radio frequencies, static discharges and the electro-magnetic pulses similar to those produced by a nuclear explosion.

But there comes a point when simulation has to stop, and the actual handling in the air of the complete aircraft and sub-systems must be assessed. This is the responsibility of the three squadrons of Test Flying and Training Divisions which provide the flying effort in support of these divisions. A Squadron flies fighters, strike and trainer aircraft; B Squadron operates bombers, tankers, maritime and transport aircraft; and D Squadron handles all helicopters irrespective of Service user. B Squadron also provides transport facilities within the United Kingdom and in support of overseas trials which are often mounted away from normal air service routes. In addition to the provision of flying effort in support of the assessment divisions, the test pilots make a unique personal contribution by their assessments which are based on specialised knowledge of the operational environment and of the suitability of aircraft for particular roles. All the pilots have recent appropriate operational backgrounds and most are graduates of perhaps the best-known of all the units at Boscombe Down: the Empire Test Pilots School (ETPS).

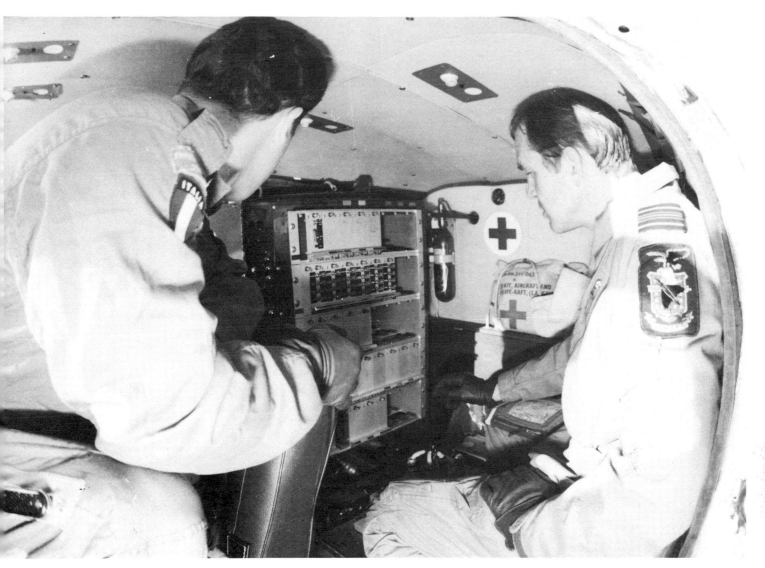

Above: A tutor at the ETPS explains the computer of the school's variable stability Basset to an overseas student test pilot.

On graduation from the School, the British pilot will either stay at Boscombe on one of the three Test Squadrons, or go to Farnborough or Bedford for other kinds of test and development flying. The steady flow of extremely highly qualified test-pilots helps to guarantee the quality of all RAF aircraft entering service and the effectiveness of subsequent in-service modifications.

The Maintenance Units

After trials have proved their effectiveness, many aircraft and other equipment modifications will be carried out at the Maintenance Units of RAF Support Command. For example, at No 30 MU at RAF Sealand all airborne radio, radar instruments and other avionics are overhauled, repaired and modified by both civilian and Service craftsmen and engineers. Over 90,000 items are dealt with each year with the aid of over £11 million worth of test equipment. St Athan, on the other hand, is responsible for the major servicing of front-line operational aircraft including Phantoms, Buccaneers, Victors, Vulcans, Canberras as well as gliders. It is also tasked with a number of supply sponsored engineering commitments. For example, it is responsible for the overhaul and repair of the Adour 102 engine and its modules, some 57 different airframe structural components from the Phantom, Buccaneer and Harrier, a wide range of fuel tanks and it also carries out the repair of the mechanical components of the Phantom, Buccaneer and Jaguar. St Athan will be the major servicing base for the Tornado.

Overall, RAF Support Command has the capability to undertake the modification, repair and servicing of almost any item held in supply depot or returned in an unserviceable condition from squadrons whenever it is expedient and economical to do so. The Command has the workshops, production lines and test facilities to service over 100,000 items a year.

Within the Command, a Field Repair Squadron is responsible for salvaging crashed RAF, Army and Navy fixed-wing aircraft in most parts of the world. The Squadron has responsibility for devising repair techniques for dealing with battle damage and also sends teams of tradesmen to operational stations to undertake aircraft modifications and repairs which are beyond the capacity of unit personnel but which do not require the aircraft to be returned to a Royal Air Force Support Command Maintenance Unit.

The Procurement Process

It is a long, complicated costly process from the first idea in an office in the Ministry of Defence to the final modification to the last production aircraft of any one type in Royal Air Force service. In the case of Tornado, it may be as long as the entire Service career of the officer who first had the idea. But along that process, the combination of imaginative forward thinking, shrewd analysis of engineering possibilities, skilful assessment of airborne characteristics and, finally, effective modification and repair techniques combine to ensure that the lifetime of the aircraft and its equipment is as productive as any military service could make it.

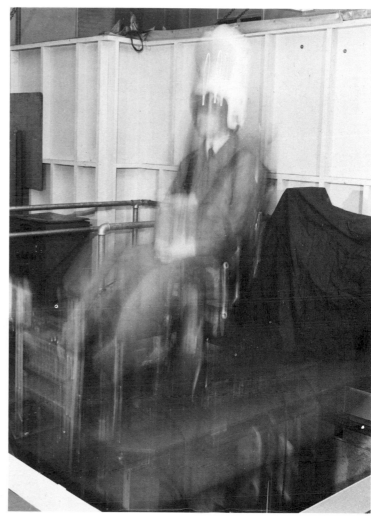

Research and Development at the Royal Aircraft Establishment

Above left: It looks like a low level beat up by a Varsity, but WL679 is a very special aeroplane based at RAE Bedford. Here it is gathering experimental data on air-to-surface target acquisition.

Inset, above left: WL679 carries Forward Looking IR (FLIR) and Low Light Level TV (LLLTV) systems in her bomb bay. The eyelid over the FLIR window protects it from debris during take-off and landing.

Left: A modified Hunter T7 is a test bed for head up display development, here fitted in parallel.

Above: An aircrew ejection seat test at RAE Farnborough with a dummy in the mockup seat.

Above right: The measurement of aircraft vibration illustrated by the blurring of the image and the pattern of the light attached to the helmet of the guinea pig. An example of the interface between man and weapons system which is probed at RAE Farnborough.

Right: The Vice Chief of the Air Staff, Air Marshal Sir David Craig, being fitted with a helmet with advanced integrated display at RAF Farnborough.

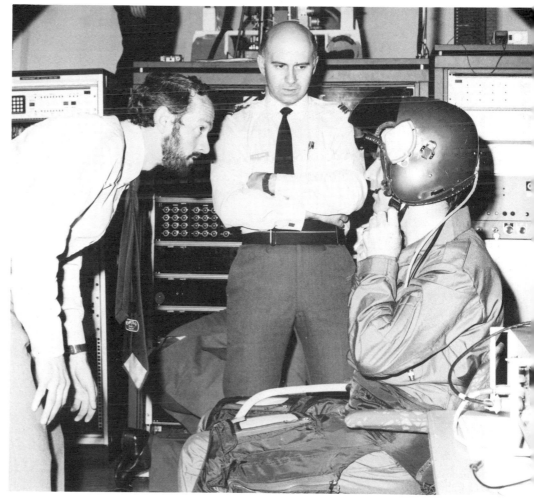

Research and Development at the Royal Signals Research Establishment

Left: Helicopter radar experiment display and control.

Below left: Unprocessed radar picture showing aircraft and extensive rain clutter; after the signal has been digitally processed (below right), plots are automatically extracted and presented. Such pictures are derived by superimposing photographically the signal from the radar over a number of aerial rotations — thus aircraft will show up as short lines of plot.

Bottom: Infra-red linescan thermal image: the discharge of warm water from a power station into the sea is clearly visible.

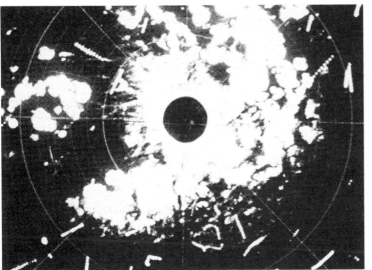

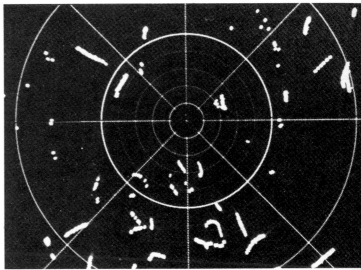

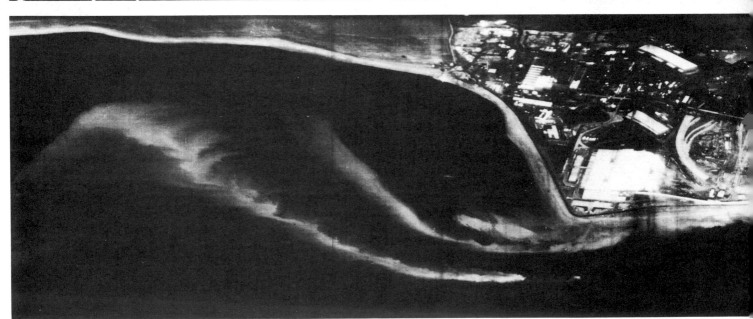

The Inventory

Left: 'For the want of a shoe . . . ' Ammunition on its way from the supply base to the front line squadron. However good the aircraft and weapon, they depend on the efficiency of the logistic chain for their effectiveness.

Below: Someone has asked for it because he needs it — the Supply Officer will ensure that it reaches him. Then perhaps she will check her existing stock against likely further demands to ensure that these also, however small, will be swiftly met.

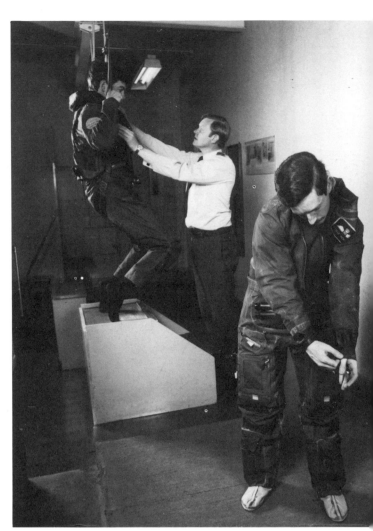
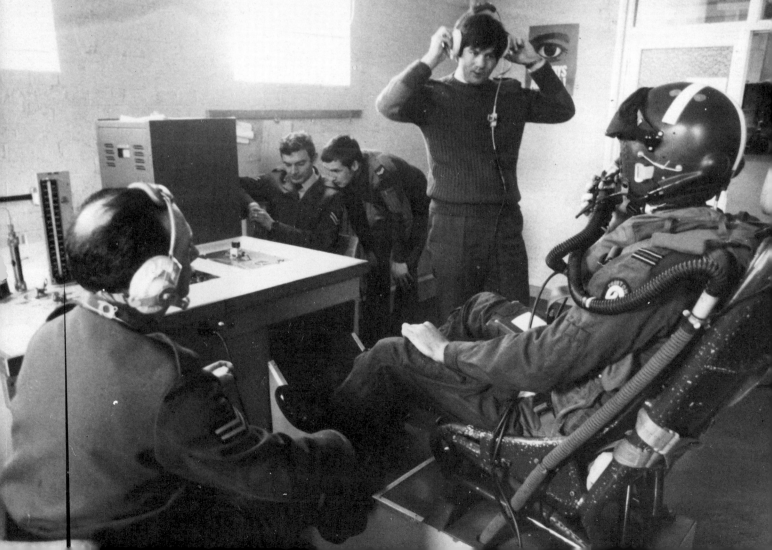

Left: A basic requirement for aircrew — apart from the aeroplane itself! — is good, well-fitting equipment. From design to final fitting (above, far left) the clothing must be able to sustain the pilot in all aspects of a most demanding environment. Individual attention is also paid to the harness (above left) and helmet (left).

Above: Among the most important items in the RAF's inventory are navigation and landing aids. The Andovers of No 115 Squadron at Brize Norton are responsible for their regular calibration.

Right: The final stage in maintaining an aircraft in line is battle damage repair. Here two airmen demonstrate that, even in NBC kit, they can patch up a fuselage well enough to be taken back into combat.

**Above: Computer control is now an essential
element in engineering and supply support.**

**Right: Third-line servicing of a Phantom — a
typical task for the maintenance units of RAF
Support Command.**

9

Operations Worldwide

Since the British withdrawal from imperial positions in the Middle and Far East, almost all operations of the RAF have become focused on NATO and Europe. 'Overseas' usually means one of the five major stations in Germany. Yet, in 1981, there were two major and one minor permanent commitments and several regular deployments well beyond the European theatre.

Belize

Until June 1973 the tiny central American territory of Belize was known as British Honduras; by then it had already received a promise of independence and was internally self-governing. But its 8,800 square miles are coveted by its much larger Western neighbour, Guatemala.

In 1975 Guatemala began to amass troops on the Belize border and reinforcement of Belize from the UK was required. Since then, British forces have been stationed in Belize as a deterrent to aggression and among them have been Harriers, helicopters and RAF Regiment units. In October 1975, three Pumas of No 33 Squadron were air-lifted to the territory, followed in November by six Harriers of No 1 Squadron which were refuelled eight times in their flight across the Atlantic. They were followed by an RAF Regiment detachment to provide airfield defence and in a

Below: Harrier of No 1 Squadron, usually based at Wittering, being towed from its inflatable hide to a jungle clearing in Belize.

very short time tension across the border lessened to such an extent that the Harriers were able to return to the United Kingdom. Regrettably, in July 1977, continued Guatemalan pressure and a repeat of the threatening gestures of two years previously prompted the United Kingdom Government to return the Harriers which, on their arrival sweep over Belize city, were greeted enthusiastically by the local population.

By 1981, although negotiations between Belize, Guatemala and the United Kingdom were again taking place, a force of 200 RAF Servicemen in a British presence of just over 2,000 remained to guarantee the small nation's integrity. The Harrier detachment was now shared between Nos 1, 3 and 4 Squadrons with four pilots on detachment at any one time. The air threat would come, if at all, from the small force of Guatemalan A-37s and the Harrier's responsibility would be to provide air defence of Belize Airport, keep open the air reinforcement routes and give close air support, reconnaissance and air cover to British ground forces. The Puma detachment, now the responsibility of No 230 Squadron, was to provide air mobility and tactical resupply to troops in an area where roads were few and movement on the ground was restricted by swamp and jungle. Regular strategic support was provided by the Lyneham Hercules Wing and the VC-10s of 10 Squadron.

When the contribution of airpower to national strategy is discussed its flexibility — the fact that it can discharge so many, responsibilities with such speed and over such distances — is frequently stressed. Its use in Belize is a small but typical example. Aircraft whose primary responsibility is to contribute to the deterrent forces facing the Warsaw Pact were deployed several thousand miles away in a matter of hours, to a climate where temperatures of 100° and very high humidity are commonplace, to act as a token of the British Government's guarantee. Moreover, although as yet not tried in combat, junior officers must accept responsibility beyond those normally faced as a squadron pilot. Under the detachment commander they will supervise the flying programme, the engine tests, flight tests, supplies and combat survival. Whereas the RAF Regiment airmen with their Rapier surface-to-air missiles will be very obvious near the main airfield, the Harriers will be deployed in the separate hides and the Pumas constantly ranging the hinterland. The result is a peace and domestic stability not shared by all the neighbours of Belize in an increasingly troubled Caribbean area.

Hong Kong

Across the other side of the world, an RAF presence is happily much more symbolic. There is no external threat to the Crown Colony of Hong Kong, now living harmoniously in the shadow of the Chinese Peoples' Republic, but there is nevertheless plenty of work to keep No 28 Squadron equipped with Westland Wessex HC2s fully occupied. Formed at Gosport in 1915, No 28 has spent all its operational service outside the UK. It flew in Italy in World War 1 and, since 1920, has operated in the Far East. It flew Lysanders, Hurricanes and Spitfires against the Japanese in Burma and moved to Hong Kong in 1949. It was successively equipped with Vampires, Venoms and Hunters at Kai Tak until assuming rotary wing duties with Whirlwind HAR10s in 1968. In 1972, it received its Wessex HC2s. In 1978, because of the increasingly congested and restricted airfield facilities at Kai Tak, the eight helicopters of the Squadron moved across into the New Territories, just four miles from the Chinese border at RAF Sek Kong. It now contributes to the continual task of the colony's ground forces in intercepting the thousands of illegal immigrants who every year seek to reach urban Hong Kong from mainland China. Rather than maintaining air surveillance it provides air mobility to the Army observation posts placed along the 22 miles of the colony's border, resupplying and rotating troops as well as evacuating casualties from positions which are frequently difficult to reach by land routes. Spotting illegal immigrants slipping across to the colony by sea is more difficult as the 55ft high speed launches tend to lose themselves among the hundreds of off-shore craft when a 28 Squadron Wessex is in the area. Again, however, as in Belize, a small number of aircraft cover a wide area in peaceful support of a civil power and give a readily visible sign of British commitment.

Below: Wessex of No 28 Squadron from Sek Kong en route to a Ghurka outpost on the mainland border with China.

Cyprus

In 1962, the skies over Cyprus were well populated by several RAF squadrons. The Canberra Wing from Akrotiri comprised Nos 6, 13, 32, 73 and 249 Squadrons. Station Flight chipped in with its own mixture of T11s and B2s; there would probably be a visiting Vulcan or Victor detachment, a couple of Canberra visitors from RAF Germany and a regular fighter squadron from the United Kingdom. The Canberras might be flying on the Episkopi or Larnaca ranges or en route to Gibraltar, Malta, Ankara, Kuwait, Aden, Peshawar, Karachi, Tehran, El Adem, Khartoum, Nairobi or Gwelo. Up the road at Nicosia, No 70 Squadron would be flying the routes East and West and No 43 Squadron would be contributing to the fighter/ground attack strength of NEAF and No 103's SAR Whirlwinds would be chattering around the Island.

By the mid-1970s, Nicosia was pockmarked by Turkish bombs, derelict and uninhabited except for a small corner occupied by the United Nations Helicopter Force. The 4,000-man strength of Akrotiri had dwindled to a handful, all but a flight of helicopters had departed and the Government was thought to be on the point of putting the Magic Bar, Heros Square, Kokkinelli and all the other traditional attractions of Aphrodite's Island out of bounds for good. Since then, however, the cost-effectiveness of the British presence on this most strategic of Mediterranean islands has been reconsidered and Akrotiri in 1980, although well short of its activity 20 years previously, had become again a very busy airfield. In its restricted 160 working hours per month it handled on average, 80 aircraft, more than 4,500 passengers and 330 tonnes of freight as well as regular detachments from squadrons in the United Kingdom and RAF Germany.

The most numerous of these comprise the nine air defence squadrons of 11 Group and RAFG arriving for their annual Armament Practice Camps (APCs). Despite the advent of the air-to-air missile, the interceptor pilot must still be able to close on an opponent and, if necessary, despatch him with guns. It will be remembered that even Tornado F2 will not be dependent solely on air-to-air missiles, however effective. Consequently Akrotiri, with its exceptionally good weather and proximity to extensive over-sea ranges, is ideally suited for air-to-air gunnery training.

In addition, the base's strategic location was utilised during Operation Agila in December 1979, when Akrotiri was a staging post for the positioning and subsequent withdrawal of troops, police and civilian administrators in Zimbabwe to supervise the ceasefire and elections. Only a few months previously the station had been the mounting and reception base for the evacuation of the British nationals from Iran.

The only permanent RAF flying squadron at Akrotiri is No 84, whose A Flight with its Whirlwind Mk10s provides traditional SAR support for the RAF visitors with two helicopters at 15-minutes standby. As is the case with SAR units in the United Kingdom, it more often comes to the rescue of civilians, both Cypriot and foreign. For example, in December 1980 a Whirlwind rescued five seamen from a Syrian coaster aground off Limassol in 50mph winds and high seas. B Flight, detached to Nicosia, is assigned for United Nations duties with the UNICYP force. Tension still exists between Turk and Greek on this often unhappy island and the Whirlwinds run regular patrols along the 'Green Line' which separates the two factions. It is most heartening to receive a friendly wave from a Greek-Cypriot post and then, a few seconds later, to acknowledge a similar greeting from the Turkish soldiers across the dividing line. Once again, a very small air force makes a contribution to peace out of all proportion to the size of its presence.

Nevada

While Lightnings and Phantoms migrate annually to the Mediterranean for hard flying in conditions perfectly suited for clear air manoeuvre and interception, Jaguars, Buccaneers and Vulcans have, since 1977, been moving in the opposite direction, across the Atlantic to an air base deep in the Nevada desert.

The reason lies in the fact that by 1975 the proportion of combat experienced crews in USAF Tactical Air Command had dropped to 30%. Yet a major lesson learned and relearned in World War 2, Korea and Vietnam had been that aircrew suffered disproportionately high losses in their first 10 combat missions but thereafter their chances of survival were higher. The Commander-in-Chief of Tactical Air Command at the time,

Below: Jaguars of No 54 Squadron, RAF Coltishall during a detachment at Nellis AFB, February 1980.

General R. J. Dickson, therefore established a novel training complex at Nellis Air Force Base which quite simply would simulate as much as possible of the environment likely to be met by USAF pilots in a future war. Since then, in a total area of nearly 4,000 square miles, a complete 'enemy' territory has been constructed.

By 1980, this 'Red Flag' training area included simulated industrial complexes, rail marshalling yards, tracks, tunnels, rolling stock, airfields, armoured divisions, supply bases and columns, command and control posts, radar stations and surface-to-air missile sites. The area is 'protected' by fighters simulating 'aggressor' tactics. The Red Flag exercises therefore cater for many kinds of offensive support, interdiction and air-to-air combat in as near real conditions as could be constructed without actual hostilities.

For example, in 1981, friendly 'Blue Forces' could expect to be faced with simulated SAM-4, 6 and 7s; 57mm, 75mm and ZSU-23mm radar-laid anti-aircraft weapons and F-5 'Fishbeds', F-106 'Floggers' and plainly hostile F-15s and F-14s depending on whose side was 'winning'.

Nor would the victor be decided by the loudest or most fluent voice in the debriefs back at Nellis at the end of the day, but by the analysis of a great deal of electronically gleaned real-time data. For example, air-to-air activity was recorded by the Cubic Corporation's Air Combat Manoeuvring Instrumentation. Video systems at the SAM and AAA sites tracked the attacking aircraft, recording both duration and range of tracking to determine the surface-to-air kill rate and also assessing the degree of destruction on the surface-to-air defences themselves by the air attacks. Simulation was actually carried through to the launch by the

Red Flag

Above left: Bowlers in the Sun! The No 208 Squadron detachment at Nellis AFB for 'Red Flag '77-9' celebrated the end of their strenuous two-week stint by donning Jubilee red, white and blue bowlers.

Left: Buccaneers of No 208 Squadron in desert camouflage during 'Red Flag '77-9'.

Above. A No 617 Squadron Vulcan framing others from Nos 35, 44, and 101 Squadrons on the Nellis AFB flightline during 'Red Flag '80-1'.

Right: Jaguars of Nos 31 and 17 Squadrons, RAFG at Nellis during a Red Flag exercise in early 1981.

Above: Another view of 31 Squadron Jaguars at Nellis.

'SAMs' of small unguided 'Smokey SAMs'; which trailed a smoke plume to about 1,000ft. Commmunication jamming from the ground completed the difficulties placed in the way of the Blue Forces tasked with one or more of the target complexes in the range.

Since August 1977, RAF squadrons have participated regularly in Red Flag exercises. In 1977, for example, Buccaneers were able to test the effectiveness of their recently installed radar warning receivers and electronic counter-measure pods. Sorties were flown at more than 500kts down to a nominal 100ft above ground level over terrain reminiscent of many a Western movie. Both cluster weapons and 1,000lb bombs were used against life-sized targets from attack runs demanding evasion from SAMs or interceptors. Buccaneer and Vulcan crews alike returned to Europe reassured about the effectiveness of their tactics and left behind a very high regard for their low level skills.

In the following year, Jaguars took part and then in November 1978, Vulcans flew night operations on the range for the first time, using terrain-following radar for long periods which also culminated in evasive manoeuvring to counter electronic warfare threats. Unlike in operations over the United Kingdom, where large amounts of tinfoil dropped from a night sky would not be well received, the Vulcans were also able to make full use of their own active ECM equipment. As before, all crews returned to the United Kingdom with increased confidence in their equipment and tactics.

Nor is experience limited to low level combat flying. The RAF squadrons participating in Red Flag do not fly independently, but as part of a composite force which may include other low level attack aircraft, 'Wild Weasel' anti-surface-to-air defence specialists and combat air patrols. Not only must the RAF aircraft co-ordinate their own sorties most closely with the others in the 'wave' — especially at night when flying without navigation lights — but the majority of pilots would have at least one chance to plan and lead the entire mission. Not surprisingly, therefore, participation in 'Red Flag' is very highly prized by Royal Air Force squadrons.

Cold Lake

Anyone who has watched a Western movie set in Nevada will realise that although the terrain might present more problems to low flying aircraft than the North German Plain, the weather is generally much kinder. Consequently, RAF participation in 1979 and 1980 in exercises several hundred miles to the north at Canadian Forces Base Cold Lake in Alberta offered more realistic climatic conditions. Exercise 'Maple Flag' is flown over several thousand square miles of almost uninhabited forest and lakeland where snow, low cloud, rain and other familiar European meteorological conditions are all too frequent. During 1980 the Canadian Forces steadily developed the facilities on the ranges. Surface-to-air missiles, vehicle and tank mock-ups were increased and plans were made to install threat simulators and electronic real-time combat analysis. In 1979 RAF Jaguars and in 1980 Harriers participated in 'Maple Flag' for the first time. Although ground threats could not be simulated as at Nellis, the plentiful availability of 'aggressor' interceptors ensured that combat conditions were realistically created.

When Canadian plans are all turned into operational equipment, Cold Lake will become an extremely valuable and most realistic training ground for RAF crews. For the Service to capitalise on Tornado GR-1's many qualities to the full, it must be flown fast and very low. The opportunity to train on ranges such as Cold Lake would not only ensure that the British taxpayer derived the greatest value from his defence spending, but that his sleep would be much less disturbed by it. Maximum effectiveness with the minimum of inconvenience may not be the most patriotic of sentiments but in a crowded island with a population quite rightly concerned with the quality of peacetime life as well as with its security, it is an important one.

And, certainly, the more efficient, the more highly trained, the more prepared for war the Royal Air Force is seen to be in the 1980s and 1990s, the less likely it is ever to be called upon to fight.

Right: A unit medical officer seeks a 'quick turnround' for a groundcrew patient — a situation typical of all unit sick quarters home and overseas.

Below: No 12 Squadron Buccaneers at RAF Gibraltar during Exercise 'Springtrain'. At extreme right is a Royal Navy Canberra.

The RAF Regiment

An airfield must be defended against attacks from the ground — and to fulfil this and other ground functions the RAF Regiment exists. Above: A mobile patrol to intercept infiltrators before they can reach ground installations.

Airmen of the Regiment could be deployed to wherever the RAF operate — from the UK (left) to Belize (right) where a Rapier unit defends an airfield.

Above right: Troops defending the perimeter fence.

Airfield security requires everything from Police (above), to firefighting and dog handling personnel (above right).

Right: Meal break for perimeter guards of the RAF Regiment.

Left: Air Vice Marshal H. Reed-Purvis OBE, Commandant-General of the RAF Regiment, presents the first armoured vehicle documents to Flt Lt Hutchinson following the reintroduction of armoured vehicles into the regiment after an absence of 25 years; and (below) one of the armoured vehicles, an Alvis Spartan APC, at RAF Catterick, headquarters of the RAF Regiment.

Appendix:

Strength of the RAF*

Role	Aircraft or Equipment	UK	RAF(G)
Strike/Attack	Vulcan B2	9 Squadron	
		35 Squadron	
		44 Squadron	
		50 Squadron	
		101 Squadron	
		617 Squadron	
	Buccaneer	12 Squadron	15 Squadron
		208 Squadron	16 Squadron
		216 Squadron	
	Jaguar		14 Squadron
			17 Squadron
			20 Squadron
			31 Squadron
Ground Support	Harrier	1 Squadron	3 Squadron
	Jaguar	6 Squadron	4 Squadron
		54 Squadron	
Maritime Patrol	Nimrod	42 Squadron	
		120 Squadron	
		201 Squadron	
		206 Squadron	
Reconnaissance	Canberra PR7	13 Squadron	
	Canberra PR9	39 Squadron	
	Vulcan SR2	27 Squadron	
	Jaguar	41 Squadron	2 Squadron
Air Defence	Lightning	5 Squadron†	
		11 Squadron†	
	Phantom FG1	43 Squadron	19 Squadron†
		111 Squadron†	92 Squadron†
	Phantom FGR2	23 Squadron†	
		29 Squadron	
		56 Squadron†	
	Bloodhound	85 Squadron†	25 Squadron †
	Rapier	27 Squadron	16 Squadron
		RAF Regiment†	RAF Regiment†
		48 Squadron	26 Squadron
		RAF Regiment†	RAF Regiment†
			37 Squadron
			RAF Regiment†
			63 Squadron
			RAF Regiment†
Airborne Early Warning	Shackleton	8 Squadron	

Role	Aircraft or Equipment	UK	RAF(G)
Air Transport	VC10	10 Squadron	
	Hercules	24 Squadron	
		30 Squadron	
		47 Squadron	
		70 Squadron	
	Wessex Helicopters	72 Squadron	18 Squadron
	Puma Helicopters	33 Squadron	
		230 Squadron	
Tanker	Victor K2	55 Squadron	
		57 Squadron	
Search and Rescue	Sea King Helicopters	202 Squadron	
	Whirlwind/Wessex Helicopters	22 Squadron	
Ground Defence	Infantry Weapons	2 Squadron RAF Regiment	1 Squadron RAF Regiment
		15 Squadron RAF Regiment	
		51 Squadron RAF Regiment	
		58 Squadron RAF Regiment	
		2503 (County of Lincoln) Squadron R Aux AF Regiment‡	
		2622 (Highland) Squadron R Aux AF Regiment‡	
		2633 (East Anglian) Squadron R Aux AF Regiment‡	

Notes:
* Normal deployment locations as at 1 Jan 1981 are shown; no
account has been taken of temporary or emergency
re-deployments. All front line aircraft, together with certain
training aircraft, are assigned to NATO or available in support of
NATO operations.
† Squadrons marked (ii) are part of NATO Command Forces.
† R Aux AF — Royal Auxiliary Air Force.
Additional deployments (outside NATO) are: one squadron of
Whirlwind helicopters and one RAF Regiment Squadron in
Cyprus; one squadron of Wessex helicopters in Hong Kong; and
a detachment of four Harriers, four Puma helicopters
and a Rapier air defence unit in Belize.

Index

Italicised page numbers indicate pictorial sectors